Copyright © 2018 by Melanie White

All rights reserved.

Published by Melanie White, www.downsizeme.net.au

Cover design and photography by Nora Wendel
www.norawendel.com

Disclaimer:

This recipe book is designed to accompany the Downsize Me Program. For more information on this program, visit www.downsizeme.net.au.

The recipes and information in this book are provided for interest and educational purposes only.

Individual nutritional needs vary considerably. This book is not intended to provide prescriptive medical or dietary advice.

Table of Contents

1 Beverages 1
Carrot, Apple and Celery Juice 2
   Detox Juice 3
   Refreshing Juice 4
2 Breakfasts 5
   Baked Quark 6
   Berry Ricotta 7
   Green Berry Smoothie 8
   Mediterranean Vegetable Frittata 9
   Omelette 10
   Scrambled Breakfast 11
   Zucchini and Leek Scramble 12
3 Soups 13
   Asian Chicken Broth 14
   Chicken and Green Veg Soup 15
   Chicken Miso Soup 16
   Chicken, Green Bean & Broccoli Soup 17
   Green Autumn Soup 18
   Lamb Immune Booster Soup 19
   Creamed Fennel Soup 20
   Vegetarian Miso Soup 21
4 Main Meals 22
   Balsamic Chicken 24
   Beef Goulash 25
   Cajun Spiced Beef and Garlicky Bean Salad 26
   Chargrilled Chicken with Asian Coleslaw 27
   Chargrilled Moroccan Lamb 28
   Chicken and Mushroom Casserole 29
   Chicken and Pea Salad 30
   Chicken and Raspberry Salad 31
   Chicken Cacciatore 32
   Chicken Ginger Curry with Green Beans and Capsicum 33
   Chicken Mediterranean 34
   Chilli Lime Chicken Salad 35
   Crab and Apple Salad 36
   Eggplant Goulash 37
   Fish and Prawn Tagine 38
   Fish, Zucchini and Oregano Bake 39
   Italian Chicken Salad 40
   Mushroom Silverbeet Frittata 41
   Parmesan Bream with Asparagus 42
   Peppered Lamb, Pea and Mint Salad 43
   Prawn and Pink Grapefruit Salad 44
   Prawn Laksa 45
   Rosemary Salmon and Asparagus 46
   San Choy Bau 47

Sate Chicken 48
Sautéed Beef in Indian Spinach Sauce 49
Savoury Baked Tofu 50
Shakshuka 51
Simple Tuna Salad 52
Slim Singapore Noodle Tofu Stir Fry 53
Spaghetti Bolognaise 54
Spanish Salad with Grilled Pork 55
Spicy Zucchini and Capsicum Eggah 56
Stuffed Beef Capsicums 57
Tamarind Chicken 58
Tamarind Tofu 59
Tofu Ginger Curry with Beans and Capsicum 60
Tofu Stir Fry 61
Tofu Tagine 62
Turkey burgers 63
Zucchini Fettuccine 64
Zucchini, Haloumi and Herb Tarts 65
5 Salad Dressings and Sauces 66
  Coconut Lime Dressing 67
  Lemon Anchovy Dressing 68
  Orange Vinaigrette 69
  Sumac and Orange Salad Dressing 70
  Vietnamese Coconut Dressing 71
6 Vegetables & salads – side dishes 72
  Asian Coleslaw 73
  Avocado, Spinach and Walnut Salad 74
  Carrot, Fennel and Apple Salad 75
  Cauliflower and Tomato Curry 76
  Eggplant with Oregano and Lemon 77
  Grated Cauliflower ('Rice') 78
  Green Bean, Tomato and Lettuce Salad 79
  Green Bean, Zucchini and Radish Stir Fry 80
  Grilled Mushroom, Tomato and Basil Salad 81
  Mashed cauliflower and sweet potato 82
  Mediterranean Salad 83
  Mexican Salsa 84
  Middle Eastern Cauliflower 85
  Mushroom Stroganoff 86
  Red Cabbage, Celery and Bokchoy Stir Fry 87
  Ricotta Salad 88
  Roasted Sweet Potato with Macadamias 89
  Semi-roasted Veg with Salsa Verde 90
  Steamed Italian Veg 91
  Streaky Spinach Salad 92
  Warm Summer Sumac Salad 93
  Zucchini Fritters 94
  Zucchini, Fennel and Mint Salad 95

7 Snacks 96
    Baked Chilli Ricotta 97
    Guacamole 98
    Roast Capsicum Dip with Green Beans 99
    Cottage Cheese Snack 100
    Lemon Passionfruit Meringue Pie 101
    Sweet Potato Truffles 102
8 Desserts 103
    Apple Snow 104
    Apple Snow, Low Fat 105
    Baked Apple 106
    Chocolate Ice Blocks 107
    Chocolate (Avocado) Mousse 108
    Lemon Slice 109
    Ricotta Apple Dream 110
    Strawberry Mousse 111

Stockists

Protein powder, Greens powder, Probiotics

Kristine Gardener, Naturopath.

+61 0419 516 127; Kristine@melbournewellnesscoaching.com.au

1 Beverages

Carrot, Apple and Celery Juice

1 medium carrot
1 green apple
4 sticks celery
1 tsp lemon juice

Procedure

1. Puree all ingredients until smooth or put through a juicer.
2. Add ice and serve immediately.

Servings: 1

Preparation Time: 5 mins; Total Time: 5 mins

Nutrition Facts

Nutrition (per serving): 175 calories, <1g total fat, 0mg cholesterol, 188.4mg sodium, 914.9mg potassium, 43.4g carbohydrates, 10.1g fibre, 30.3g sugar, 2.4g protein.

Detox Juice

1 whole apple, chopped
1 sprig parsley
3 stalks celery
1/2 whole lemon
1/2 whole cucumber

Procedure

1. Remove the peel from the lemon. Roughly chop all ingredients.
2. Blend with ice until smooth and creamy, or put through a juicer and add ice.

Preparation Time: 5 mins; Total Time: 5 mins

Servings: 1

Nutrition Facts

Nutrition (per serving): 121 calories, <1g total fat, 0mg cholesterol, 113.7mg sodium, 755.6mg potassium, 29.2g carbohydrates, 7.4g fibre, 19.7g sugar, 2.6g protein.

Recipe Tip

Using a blender will preserve the pulp and fibre.

Refreshing Juice

3 whole cucumbers
1 whole apple, chopped
1 sprig parsley
1 whole carrot
1 tbsp lemon juice, freshly squeezed

Procedure

1. Blend with ice until smooth or put all ingredients through a juicer, then add ice. Serve immediately.

Servings: 1

Preparation Time: 5 mins; Total Time: 5 mins

Nutrition Facts

Nutrition (per serving): 230 calories, 2.1g total fat, 0mg cholesterol, 71.4mg sodium, 1730.1mg potassium, 51.5g carbohydrates, 13.5g fibre, 32.1g sugar, 7.2g protein.

Recipe Tips

A carrot can be added for a different flavour in Phase 3. Using a blender will preserve the pulp and fibre.

2 Breakfasts

Baked Quark

200 grams light quark (or ricotta), low fat

1 egg white

1 sprig chives, finely chopped

2 sprigs basil leaves, chopped

Procedure

1. Preheat oven to 180 degrees C and brush a one-cup ramekin dish with a little coconut oil (or spray oil).
2. Combine all ingredients and mix well. Season with salt and pepper (optional).
3. Spoon mixture into ramekin and smooth the surface.
4. Bake for 25 mins or until golden and set.
5. Serve immediately.

Servings: 1

Preparation Time: 5 mins; Cooking Time: 25 mins; Total Time: 30 mins

Nutrition Facts

Nutrition (per serving): 187 calories, <1g total fat, 18mg cholesterol, 375.8mg sodium, 319mg potassium, 6.3g carbohydrates, <1g fibre, 6.1g sugar, 31.9g protein.

Berry Ricotta

1/2 cup mixed berries (or a whole orange, peeled)

125 grams ricotta or cottage cheese, light

1 pinch cinnamon

1 pinch stevia (optional)

Procedure

1. Place peeled orange in a bowl and top with ricotta.
2. Sprinkle over cinnamon and, if desired, stevia.

Servings: 1

Preparation Time: 5 mins; Total Time: 5 mins

Nutrition Facts

Nutrition (per serving): 132 calories, 1.5g total fat, 5mg cholesterol, 508.3mg sodium, 164.6mg potassium, 14.1g carbohydrates, 1.9g fibre, 10.6g sugar, 16g protein.

Recipe Tip

1 tsp of chia pudding can be a nice addition.

Green Berry Smoothie

1 cup blueberries or mixed berries
1 scoop protein powder*
1 scoop Greens powder**
1 sachet probiotic (optional)
1 pinch stevia (or to taste)
3/4 cup water

Procedure

1 Blend all ingredients until smooth.
2 Serve immediately.

Servings: 1

Preparation Time: 5 mins; Total Time: 5 mins

Nutrition Facts

Nutrition (per serving): 173 calories, <1g total fat, 0mg cholesterol, 21.8mg sodium, 303.4mg potassium, 31g carbohydrates, 7.5g fibre, 15.4g sugar, 12.6g protein.

* Choose plain whey or soy protein isolate protein powder, or plain greens powder, without any added sugars, colours, flavours or other ingredients. For specific brand advice, contact info@downsizeme.net.au.

** Greens powder is a generic term that refers to any 'greens' supplement powder. Common commercial brands include Super Greens, Organic Greens, etc.

Mediterranean Vegetable Frittata

1/2 tsp coconut oil
1 whole egg, lightly beaten
3 whole egg whites, lightly beaten
1 sprig parsley, chopped
3 halves tomato, semi-dried, sliced
1/2 whole red bell pepper, julienned
1 whole zucchini, grated
2 cups spinach leaves
100 grams mushrooms, chopped
50 grams ricotta cheese, extra light

Procedure

1. Preheat the oven to 180 degrees C.
2. Use the coconut oil to grease a pie or flan dish.
3. Combine eggs with the fresh herbs and prepared vegetables.
4. Stir in ricotta cheese.
5. Pour mixture into the dish and bake for about 20 mins, until firm.

Servings: 1

Preparation Time: 5 mins; Cooking Time: 20 mins; Total Time: 25 mins

Nutrition Facts

Nutrition (per serving): 324 calories, 12.8g total fat, 201.5mg cholesterol, 387.4mg sodium, 1870.7mg potassium, 23.9g carbohydrates, 6.9g fibre, 14.2g sugar, 31.9g protein.

Recipe Tip

Can be cooked in a non-stick frypan with a lid, instead of the oven.

Omelette

3 large egg whites, lightly beaten
1 tbsp hot water
30 grams Spanish onion, finely chopped
1 sprig basil, chopped

Procedure

1. Whisk egg whites until frothy; add 1 tbsp hot water and whisk to combine.
2. Dry fry the onions in a non-stick pan.
3. Put the heat down to low, add the egg whites, and cook until just set.
4. Serve with fresh basil.

Servings: 1

Preparation Time: 5 mins; Cooking Time: 5 mins; Total Time: 10 mins

Nutrition Facts

Nutrition (per serving): 62 calories, <1g total fat, 0mg cholesterol, 165.7mg sodium, 169.3mg potassium, 3.1g carbohydrates, <1g fibre, <1g sugar, 11.2g protein.

Recipe Tips

Hot water makes the eggs fluffier.
Putting a lid on the pan to set the top makes the eggs fluffier.
Asparagus and capsicum make a tasty topping.

Scrambled Breakfast

3 large egg whites, lightly beaten

1 tbsp hot water

100 grams mushrooms, sliced

50 grams spinach leaves

30 grams onions, diced

1 sprig parsley, finely chopped (optional)

Procedure

1. Whisk egg whites until frothy; add 1 tbsp hot water and whisk through.
2. Heat a non-stick pan to medium, sauté mushroom and onion until lightly cooked.
3. Turn stove to low heat and add egg whites to pan.
4. Stir through spinach leaves just before the egg is set.
5. Serve immediately; garnish with fresh herbs if desired.

Servings: 1

Preparation Time: 5 mins; Cooking Time: 5 mins; Total Time: 10 mins

Nutrition Facts

Nutrition (per serving): 97 calories, <1g total fat, 0mg cholesterol, 211.1mg sodium, 808.2mg potassium, 8.7g carbohydrates, 2.7g fibre, 4.2g sugar, 15.7g protein.

Zucchini and Leek Scramble

1 small leek, white only, chopped

1 medium zucchini, unpeeled, and grated

1/2 cup mushrooms, sliced

1/2 cup cabbage, shredded

1/2 cup silverbeet (chard), raw, chopped

2 egg whites, lightly beaten

Procedure

1. Heat a non-stick pan over medium and dry fry the leeks, mushrooms and zucchini until golden.
2. Add the cabbage and stir through until just heated.
3. Add the egg whites and stir through until cooked.
4. Top with fresh basil and oregano and serve.

Servings: 1

Preparation Time: 10 mins; Total Time: 10 mins

Nutrition Facts

Nutrition (per serving): 147 calories, 1.3g total fat, 0mg cholesterol, 193.1mg sodium, 1077.2mg potassium, 24g carbohydrates, 5.4g fibre, 11.4g sugar, 13.4g protein.

3 Soups

Asian Chicken Broth

100 grams chicken breast halves, skinned, diced
100 grams cabbage, shredded
100 grams zucchini, thinly sliced
5 ml Herbamare vegetable stock powder
475 ml water
2 stalks celery chopped
50 grams leeks thinly sliced
50 grams bell pepper, chopped
50 grams radish
1 tbsp coriander
1 stalk lemon grass
1 clove garlic clove, minced

Procedure

1. Chop leeks and garlic and dry sauté in a heavy saucepan.
2. Add chicken to the pot; stir quickly to avoid sticking (add water as needed).
3. Add remaining ingredients except stock; stir fry until golden.
4. Add 2 cups of water and stock powder) to the pot, stir well, simmer and reduce for about 30 mins.
5. Top with fresh coriander and ground pepper if desired.

Servings: 1

Preparation Time: 10 mins; Cooking Time: 30 mins; Total Time: 40 mins

Nutrition Facts

Nutrition (per serving): 296 calories, 5.1g total fat, 85mg cholesterol, 765.1mg sodium, 1342.3mg potassium, 27.6g carbohydrates, 8.7g fibre, 13g sugar, 36.4g protein.

Chicken and Green Veg Soup

100 grams chicken breasts -- boned and skinned

50 grams green beans

50 grams spinach leaves

30 grams fennel bulbs

0.5 can tomato, diced

2 stalks celery

1 clove garlic

5 ml oregano leaves

75 ml vegetable stock (e.g. Herbamare)

Procedure

1. Chop all vegetables finely and mince garlic.
2. Heat a soup pot; add a little water and sauté garlic, fennel and celery for 3 - 4 mins.
3. Add 75 mL liquid stock (or 1/2 tsp powder in 75mL water), cover and simmer for a few mins on low heat.
4. Add tomatoes, pre-cooked chicken, beans and herbs.
5. Simmer for 30 mins over low heat.

Servings: 1

Preparation Time: 5 mins; Cooking Time: 40 mins; Total Time: 45 mins

Nutrition Facts

Nutrition (per serving): 189 calories, 3.3g total fat, 64mg cholesterol, 519mg sodium, 1320.8mg potassium, 15.5g carbohydrates, 6.3g fibre, 5.9g sugar, 25.6g protein.

Recipe Tip

Use leftover chicken to make this dish.

Chicken Miso Soup

1/2 tsp coconut oil
100 grams chicken breast, cooked and chopped
15 ml miso soup paste
150 ml boiling water
50 grams mushrooms
50 grams capsicum, red, chopped
30 grams tomato, diced
1 whole spring onion, finely chopped

Procedure

1. Heat coconut oil in the pan and reheat the cooked chicken.
2. Add mushrooms and capsicum, stir well, cook for 5 mins.
3. Add tomato and stir through.
4. Add miso paste and boiling water.
5. Simmer for 10 mins.
6. Pour into a bowl and top with spring onions. Serve immediately.

Servings: 1

Preparation Time: 5 mins; Cooking Time: 20 mins; Total Time: 25 mins

Nutrition Facts

Nutrition (per serving): 226 calories, 6.4g total fat, 85mg cholesterol, 408.4mg sodium, 653.4mg potassium, 7.6g carbohydrates, 2.6g fibre, 4.4g sugar, 33.8g protein.

Chicken, Green Bean & Broccoli Soup

1 clove garlic clove, chopped
100 grams leek, white only, chopped
120 grams chicken breast, diced
1 tsp Herbamare vegetable stock powder in water
100 ml water
50 grams green beans, trimmed and cut in half
50 grams broccoli florets, cut into small pieces
2 stalks celery, diced
1 sprig basil leaves, chopped
1 tbsp parsley, finely chopped

Procedure

1. Heat a non-stick pan to medium heat and dry fry garlic and leek. Lower heat, brown chicken.
2. In the meantime, heat stock powder and water. Add chopped vegetables, and then add garlic, leek and chicken.
3. Simmer on low heat for 10 mins.
4. Add chopped herbs and simmer for a further 5 mins.
5. Serve immediately.

Servings: 1

Preparation Time: 10 mins; Cooking Time: 15 mins; Total Time: 25 mins

Nutrition Facts

Nutrition (per serving): 251 calories, 4g total fat, 76.8mg cholesterol, 526.4mg sodium, 1185.4mg potassium, 24.7g carbohydrates, 4.9g fibre, 7.6g sugar, 30.5g protein.

Recipe Tip

Blend soup for creamy broth or add slim pasta noodles for variety.

Green Autumn Soup

1 tsp extra virgin olive oil
1 clove garlic clove, finely chopped
1 medium carrot, finely grated
2 stalks celery, finely grated
1 bunch cabbage, Asian (bokchoy), finely diced
2 cups stock
120 grams chicken breast, cooked, diced

Procedure

1. Lightly fry garlic, carrot and celery in the olive oil.
2. Add the bokchoy and stir through, then add the stock.
3. Simmer on low heat for 10 mins.
4. Add chopped chicken and simmer for a further 5 mins, then serve.

Servings: 1

Preparation Time: 10 mins; Cooking Time: 15 mins; Total Time: 25 mins

Nutrition Facts

Nutrition (per serving): 297 calories, 8.6g total fat, 76.8mg cholesterol, 1272.5mg sodium, 2037.9mg potassium, 17.6g carbohydrates, 4.3g fibre, 8.4g sugar, 37.9g protein.

Recipe Tips

Blend soup for creamy broth or add slim pasta noodles for variety.

Lamb Immune Booster Soup

100 grams leeks thinly sliced
1 clove garlic clove, crushed
100 grams lamb cutlet, diced
100 grams silverbeet (chard), raw, chopped
100 grams broccoli florets
2 tsp Herbamare vegetable stock powder
1 stalk celery, finely chopped
1 tbsp parsley, finely chopped
1 sprig rosemary, fresh, chopped
1 tsp oregano, chopped
1 pinch black pepper freshly ground
3 cups water

Procedure

1. Dry sauté the leek and garlic in a pot.
2. Add the lamb; cook quickly without turning, until just brown on one side.
3. Add remaining ingredients and stir quickly; add the water and stock powder.
4. Simmer for 20 - 25 mins.

Servings: 1

Preparation Time:15 mins; Cooking Time: 25 mins; Total Time: 40 mins

Nutrition Facts

Nutrition (per serving): 347 calories, 15.9g total fat, 66mg cholesterol, 1471.6mg sodium, 1449.9mg potassium, 28.8g carbohydrates, 5.5g fibre, 7.1g sugar, 25.8g protein.

Recipe Tips

Blend the soup if desired for a thicker consistency.

Creamed Fennel Soup

1/2 whole avocado
2 stalks celery
75 grams fennel bulbs
1 whole spring onion
3 tbsp lemon juice
1 pinch Himalayan salt
1 pinch black pepper freshly ground, to taste
2 sprigs coriander

Procedure

1. Blend all ingredients until smooth and creamy.
2. Add water and fresh herbs to achieve the desired consistency and flavour.

Servings: 1

Preparation Time: 10 mins; Total Time: 10 mins

Nutrition Facts

Nutrition (per serving): 227 calories, 15.4g total fat, 0mg cholesterol, 416mg sodium, 1221.7mg potassium, 25g carbohydrates, 11.6g fibre, 5.1g sugar, 4.4g protein.

Vegetarian Miso Soup

1 tbsp miso soup paste
150 ml vegetable stock
50 grams mushrooms
75 grams cabbage, Asian (bokchoy or pakchoy), shredded
30 grams radish, finely chopped
100 grams tofu, cubed (2cm)
1 whole spring onion, finely chopped

Procedure

1. Heat miso paste with stock; add whole mushrooms and simmer until mushrooms are soft.
2. Add the tofu, radish and cabbage to the soup base.
3. Cook for 1 - 2 mins, then pour into a bowl and top with spring onions.

Servings: 1

Preparation Time: 5 mins; Cooking Time: 20 mins; Total Time: 25 mins

Nutrition Facts

Nutrition (per serving): 117 calories, 6.3g total fat, 0mg cholesterol, 379.9mg sodium, 470.9mg potassium, 6.6g carbohydrates, 2.1g fibre, 2.7g sugar, 12.2g protein.

4 Main Meals

Asparagus and Leek Quiche

2 sticks grissini stick
100 grams leeks, chopped
3 egg whites, lightly beaten
1 sprig rosemary, fresh, chopped
1 sprig thyme leaves
50 grams asparagus, cut in 1-inch pieces
4 whole cherry tomatoes, halved

Procedure

1. Preheat oven to 180 degrees C.
2. Line a small ramekin dish with baking paper.
3. Finely crumble grissini stick into the dish, and drizzle with a little water to soften crumbs. Press firmly together.
4. Arrange sliced leeks on top.
5. Whisk egg whites with herbs; pour over leeks.
6. Top with asparagus and cherry tomatoes.
7. Bake for 15 mins or until cooked through.
8. Serve with a fresh green salad.

Servings: 1

Preparation Time: 10 mins; Cooking Time: 15 mins; Total Time: 25 mins

Nutrition Facts

Nutrition (per serving): 182 calories, 1.8g total fat, 0mg cholesterol, 265.3mg sodium, 623.9mg potassium, 27.3g carbohydrates, 4.2g fibre, 5.7g sugar, 15.4g protein.

Balsamic Chicken

120 grams chicken breast halves, cut into 3/4-inch pieces
1 tbsp balsamic vinegar
1 clove garlic, minced
1 sprig tarragon leaves
1 pinch black pepper freshly ground, to taste

Procedure

1. Combine the balsamic vinegar, garlic and pepper then pour over chicken breasts and marinate for 10 mins.
2. Heat a barbecue grill to medium high.
3. Cook the chicken for approximately 5 - 7 mins on each side until chicken is cooked through. Serve with vegetables.

Servings: 1

Preparation Time: 10 mins; Cooking Time: 15 mins; Total Time: 25 mins

Nutrition Facts

Nutrition (per serving): 205 calories, 4.2g total fat, 76.8mg cholesterol, 152.3mg sodium, 925.6mg potassium, 10.1g carbohydrates, <1g fibre, 2.4g sugar, 29g protein.

Recipe Tip

This dish is delicious with Mediterranean Salad (page 83), salsa and squash.

Beef Goulash

120 grams rump steak, cubed
1 clove garlic, minced
1 small onion, diced
100 grams mushrooms, sliced
100 grams capsicum, red, chopped
1 tsp paprika
1 bay leaf
1/2 cup beef stock
1 whole tomato, diced
1 tbsp coconut cream
1 sprig parsley, chopped
1 serve Slim Pasta

Procedure

1. Preheat oven to 180 degrees C.
2. Heat a large, flame-proof casserole dish on medium high heat.
3. Cook beef in the dish for 5 - 6 mins until brown, then place in a bowl.
4. Add onion, garlic, mushrooms and capsicum. Cook for 5 mins or until onion has softened, stirring regularly.
5. Return beef to the dish, add paprika. Stir, add bay leaf.
6. Stir in stock and tomato. Cover dish and bring to the boil.
7. Transfer dish to the oven; bake 1 - 2 hours until beef is tender.
8. Spoon 1/4 cup of liquid from the cooked goulash into a bowl. Add coconut cream; stir until smooth and combined.
9. Add the coconut mix to the goulash and stir to combine.
10. Drain a portion of Slim Pasta and soak in boiling water for 2 mins. Drain again and add to a bowl, top with the goulash, and sprinkle with chopped parsley.

Servings: 1

Preparation Time: 20 mins; Cooking Time: 2 hrs; Total Time: 2hrs and 20 mins

Nutrition Facts

Nutrition (per serving): 326 calories, 12.3g total fat, 49.2mg cholesterol, 335mg sodium, 1119.9mg potassium, 23.1g carbohydrates, 6.3g fibre, 11.7g sugar, 35g protein.

Cajun Spiced Beef and Garlicky Bean Salad

1 clove garlic, minced (dressing)

1 tsp lemon juice (dressing)

1 tsp wholegrain mustard (dressing)

120 grams beef steak, extra lean

1 tsp Cajun spice

30 grams Spanish onion, finely chopped

100 grams green beans

100 grams cucumber, sliced

1 sprig coriander leaves

Procedure

1. Make dressing by combining lemon juice, garlic and mustard. Set aside.
2. Sprinkle beef on both sides with Cajun spice mix, and grill on the barbecue. Remove from heat, stand 5 mins, then slice thinly.
3. Combine remaining ingredients in a bowl with dressing. Toss, then serve to a plate and top with beef.

Servings: 1

Preparation Time: 5 mins; Cooking Time: 7 mins; Total Time: 12 mins

Nutrition Facts

Nutrition (per serving): 205 calories, 6g total fat, 41mg cholesterol, 360.3mg sodium, 391.9mg potassium, 15.4g carbohydrates, 4.6g fibre, 4.8g sugar, 25.6g protein.

Chargrilled Chicken with Asian Coleslaw

120 grams chicken breasts
1 tbsp soy sauce
1 clove garlic, minced
1 tsp ginger, freshly grated
3 pinches stevia
1 pinch chili flakes
200 grams cabbage, Asian (bokchoy), shredded
1 spring onion, finely chopped
2 sprigs coriander leaves
1 serve Coconut Lime Dressing
1/2 whole lime, quartered (garnish)
1 sprig coriander leaves (garnish)
1 whole chili, chopped (garnish)

Procedure

1. Place chicken in a bowl with soy, ginger, garlic, stevia and chili flakes. Mix well and marinate for 10 mins.
2. Toss the cabbage, spring onions and coriander in a bowl with Coconut Lime Dressing, then chill the salad.
3. Heat the barbecue grill to medium and cook the chicken through, stand for a few minutes and then slice.
4. Top the salad with the chicken slices.
5. Garnish with lime wedges, fresh coriander and fresh cut chili.

Servings: 1

Preparation Time: 10 mins; Cooking Time: 15 mins; Inactive Time: 10 mins; Total Time: 35 mins

Nutrition Facts

Nutrition (per serving): 284 calories, 10.3g total fat, 76.8mg cholesterol, 832.2mg sodium, 1411mg potassium, 20.8g carbohydrates, 5g fibre, 6.7g sugar, 31.9g protein.

Recipe Tip

This dish also goes well with Grated Cauliflower (Rice) (Page 78).

Chargrilled Moroccan Lamb

75 grams sweet potato, cubed
100 grams lamb cutlets
1 tsp Moroccan seasoning
2 cups rocket leaves
20 grams feta cheese, crumbled
50 grams red capsicum, cut into strips
1 tsp pine nuts
2 sprigs basil leaves, chopped

Procedure
1. Grill the sweet potato cubes in a non-stick pan, turning regularly until cooked through. Set aside.
2. Sprinkle lamb cutlets with Moroccan spice and chargrill over medium heat for 3 - 4 mins each side, or until cooked to your liking. Cover with foil to keep warm if required.
3. Arrange rocket on a plate. Add the cubed feta and capsicum, then scatter sweet potato over the top.
4. Serve with lamb chops and garnish with pine nuts and basil leaves.

Servings: 1

Preparation Time: 10 mins; Cooking Time: 10 mins; Total Time: 20 mins

Nutrition Facts
Nutrition (per serving): 379 calories, 21.5g total fat, 83.8mg cholesterol, 340.1mg sodium, 896.2mg potassium, 21.8g carbohydrates, 4.4g fibre, 7g sugar, 24.8g protein.

Acknowledgement
Image supplied by Kerry Meek

Chicken and Mushroom Casserole

1 tsp olive oil
150 grams chicken breast, cut into strips
1 small onion, finely diced
100 grams mushrooms, sliced
1 tsp Dijon mustard
100 ml chicken stock
1 tbsp coconut cream, or avocado puree
1 pinch Himalayan salt
1 pinch black pepper freshly ground
1 tbsp parsley, chopped

Procedure

1. Heat oil in a large frying pan over medium high heat. Cook chicken for 5 mins or until golden; transfer to a plate.
2. Add onion to the pan. Cook for 3 - 4 mins; add mushrooms and cook for another 2 mins.
3. Stir in mustard and cook, stirring, for another 2 mins.
4. Gradually stir in stock and bring to the boil.
5. Return chicken to the pan, cover, reduce heat to low and simmer for about 10 mins.
6. Remove from heat; add coconut cream and stir through quickly; season with salt and pepper.
7. Stir in parsley, then serve.

Servings: 1

Preparation Time: 10 mins; Cooking Time: 15 mins; Total Time: 25 mins

Nutrition Facts

Nutrition (per serving): 461 calories, 26g total fat, 119.6mg cholesterol, 808.4mg sodium, 1261.3mg potassium, 15g carbohydrates, 2.7g fibre, 6.8g sugar, 42.2g protein.

Chicken and Pea Salad

160 grams chicken breasts
100 grams snow peas, chopped in half
2 cups lettuce, shredded
150 grams sweet potato, peeled and cubed
1 tbsp walnut halves
1 sprig parsley, chopped
1 sprig basil leaves, chopped
1 tsp sunflower seeds, lightly toasted and chopped

Procedure

1. Cook chicken and sweet potato on a medium heat barbecue grill or non-stick frypan, until cooked through.
2. Slice chicken thinly.
3. Add chicken and sweet potato cubes to remaining ingredients and toss well.
4. Sprinkle with toasted, chopped sunflower seeds (optional).

Servings: 1

Preparation Time: 5 mins Cooking Time: 15 mins Total Time: 20 mins

Nutrition Facts

Nutrition (per serving): 434 calories, 10.8g total fat, 102.4mg cholesterol, 293.8mg sodium, 1522mg potassium, 42.8g carbohydrates, 9.2g fibre, 12.7g sugar, 41.9g protein.

Recipe Tip

Use leftover chicken and sweet potato to make this meal even quicker.

Chicken and Raspberry Salad

160 grams chicken breasts
1/2 tsp coconut oil
1 cup lettuce, shredded
1 cup kale, finely chopped
1 cup spinach leaves
1 whole red bell pepper cut into 1/4-inch cubes
1 tbsp walnut halves
2 tbsp raspberry vinegar
100 grams raspberries

Procedure

1. Heat coconut oil in a non-stick frypan on medium heat. Cook chicken until browned and cooked through.
2. Combine washed greens and berries with chicken breast (whole or sliced).
3. Sprinkle with walnuts and raspberry vinegar.
4. Serve immediately.

Servings: 1

Preparation Time: 10 mins Cooking Time: 20 mins Total Time: 30 mins

Nutrition Facts

Nutrition (per serving): 399 calories, 13.2g total fat, 102.4mg cholesterol, 247.5mg sodium, 1686.2mg potassium, 32.1g carbohydrates, 11.4g fibre, 11.9g sugar, 42g protein.

Recipe Tip

Use leftover cooked chicken for a quick option.

Chicken Cacciatore

120 grams chicken breasts
1 pinch Himalayan salt
1 pinch black pepper
150 grams tomato puree
30 grams brown onions, diced
1 clove garlic, chopped
1 medium red bell pepper seeded and chopped
75 grams mushrooms, sliced
1 sprig basil leaves, chopped
1 tsp rosemary, fresh, chopped
1 tbsp parsley, finely chopped
100 ml chicken stock, home made

Procedure

1. Season chicken breast with pepper and salt, brown in a non-stick pan on medium heat.
2. Add remaining vegetables and herbs, stirring quickly for up to 1 minute.
3. Add stock and simmer for at least 30 mins or until chicken is cooked through.

Servings: 1

Preparation Time: 10 mins; Cooking Time: 30 mins; Total Time: 40 mins

Nutrition Facts

Nutrition (per serving): 261 calories, 4.8g total fat, 67mg cholesterol, 1348.5mg sodium, 1561.2mg potassium, 26g carbohydrates, 6.5g fibre, 15.8g sugar, 30.1g protein.

Chicken Ginger Curry with Green Beans and Capsicum

1 tsp coriander, ground
1 sprig basil leaves
1 clove garlic
1 stalk lemongrass
1 tsp cumin seeds
1 small chili pepper
1 tsp ginger root
1 tsp tamari
1 tsp lime juice
1/2 Spanish onion
20 ml coconut milk
120 grams chicken breasts
1 leaf Kafir lime
100 grams green beans
1 whole red bell pepper, diced

Procedure

1. Make curry paste by processing or blending all herbs (except Kefir leaf) with garlic, onion, ginger, tamari.
2. Add coconut milk and process again.
3. Heat a non-stick pan to medium and stir fry the paste until fragrant (about 1 min). Add chicken, stir to combine, cook chicken through.
4. Add lime leaves and reduce heat to low, cover and simmer, stirring occasionally, for about 5 mins.
5. Add red capsicum and beans, stir and cook for 2 - 3 mins, until beans are bright green. Increase saltiness with 1 tsp of tamari or decrease saltiness with a little fresh lime juice.

Servings: 1

Prep. Time: 5 mins; Cooking Time: 20 mins; Total Time: 25 mins

Nutrition Facts

Nutrition (per serving): 283 calories, 8.7g total fat, 76.8mg cholesterol, 497.8mg sodium, 1064.6mg potassium, 23.5g carbs, 5.7g fibre, 6g sugar, 31g protein.

Recipe Tip

Vegetable stock can be used to increase sauce volume.

Chicken Mediterranean

120 grams chicken breasts
1 clove garlic
100 grams capsicum, finely chopped
100 grams cherry tomatoes, halved
100 grams spinach leaves
1 sprig rosemary, finely chopped
1 sprig parsley, flat-leaved, chopped
3 tbsp chives, finely chopped

Procedure

1. Mince fresh garlic and spread over chicken breast, grill/ BBQ.
2. While chicken is cooking, prepare vegetables and herbs, toss well.
3. Plate up the salad and herbs and top with cooked chicken.

Servings: 1

Preparation Time: 5 mins; Cooking Time: 25 mins; Total Time: 30 mins

Nutrition Facts

Nutrition (per serving): 247 calories, 4.9g total fat, 92.2mg cholesterol, 260.1mg sodium, 1559.9mg potassium, 15.6g carbohydrates, 5.8g fibre, 4.8g sugar, 35.7g protein.

Chilli Lime Chicken Salad

150 ml chicken stock, home made
30 ml water
160 grams chicken breast halves
100 grams capsicum, finely chopped
75 grams bokchoy, shredded
30 grams radish, red
1 cup bean sprouts
1 sprig coriander, finely chopped
1 tbsp chives, finely chopped
1 pinch stevia (for dressing)
1 clove garlic, minced (for dressing)
1 small green chili peppers, chopped (for dressing)
1 tsp fish sauce (for dressing)
1 tbsp lime juice (for dressing)

Procedure

1. Bring water and stock to the boil over medium heat. Add chicken, reduce heat and simmer for about 10 mins to cook through.
2. Toss cabbage, capsicum, coriander, radish, chives and bean sprouts.
3. Remove chicken from heat and cool chicken in pan about 10 mins, then slice thinly.
4. Make the chilli lime dressing by combining lime juice, stevia, chilli and garlic in the pan you used to cook the chicken. Stir over low heat for a few mins, then cool. Stir through fish sauce when the dressing has cooled.
5. Plate salad, top with chicken and drizzle with dressing.

Servings: 1

Preparation Time: 10 mins; Cooking Time: 10 mins; Total Time: 20 mins

Nutrition Facts

Nutrition (per serving): 351 calories, 6.8g total fat, 106.5mg cholesterol, 1150.6mg sodium, 1290.2mg potassium, 25.5g carbohydrates, 5.3g fibre, 14.4g sugar, 47.5g protein.

Crab and Apple Salad

1 tbsp lime juice (dressing)
1 tsp fish sauce (dressing)
1 tsp coconut oil (dressing)
2 pinches stevia (dressing)
1 whole chili (chopped, dressing)
1 whole apple, cored and chopped
1 serve Slim Pasta
120 grams crab meat, boiled or grilled
2 cups lettuce, mixed, shredded
20 grams Spanish onion, chopped
1/4 avocados, small, chopped
2 sprigs coriander leaves (garnish)

Procedure

1. Make chili dressing by mixing lime juice, fish sauce, coconut oil, fresh chili and stevia.
2. Mix chopped apple with lettuce, avocado, onion and crab meat.
3. Drain Slim Pasta and soak in boiling water for 2 mins, drain and add to salad.
4. Toss through dressing and garnish with fresh coriander.

Servings: 1

Preparation Time: 10 mins; Total Time: 10 mins

Nutrition Facts

Nutrition (per serving): 338 calories, 13.5g total fat, 116.4mg cholesterol, 964mg sodium, 1185.8mg potassium, 33.1g carbohydrates, 9.2g fibre, 18.6g sugar, 25.9g protein.

Eggplant Goulash

120 grams eggplant, sliced into lengthways strips
1 clove garlic, minced
1 small onion, diced
2 egg whites, beaten
100 grams mushrooms, sliced
100 grams capsicum, chopped
1 tsp paprika
1 bay leaf
1/2 cup beef stock
1 whole tomato, diced
1 tbsp coconut milk
1 sprig parsley, chopped
1 serve Slim Pasta

Procedure

1. Preheat oven to 180 degrees C.
2. Heat a large, flame-proof casserole dish on medium high heat.
3. Cook eggplant slices for 5 mins, until brown. Transfer to bowl.
4. Add onion, garlic, mushrooms and capsicum. Cook for 5 mins or until onion has softened, stirring regularly.
5. Return eggplant to the dish, add paprika, stir, add bay leaf.
6. Stir in stock and tomato. Cover dish and bring to the boil.
7. Stir egg whites through; bake until veg are tender (10 mins).
8. Spoon 1/4 cup of liquid from the cooked goulash into a bowl. Add coconut cream; stir until smooth and combined.
9. Add the coconut mix to the goulash and stir to combine.
10. Drain one portion of Slim Pasta and soak in boiling water for 2 mins. Drain and add to a bowl, top with the goulash, and sprinkle with chopped parsley.

Servings: 1

Preparation Time: 10 mins; Cooking Time: 25 mins; Total Time: 35 mins

Nutrition Facts

Nutrition (per serving): 234 calories, 6.8g total fat, 0mg cholesterol, 369.1mg sodium, 1503.6mg potassium, 30.6g carbohydrates, 9.9g fibre, 16.4g sugar, 17.3g protein.

Fish and Prawn Tagine

1 clove garlic, crushed (marinade)
2 tsp lemon juice (marinade)
1/2 tsp ground cumin (marinade)
1 sprig coriander, chopped (marinade)
30 ml water (marinade)
100 grams whiting fillets
1 whole Spanish onion, finely chopped (sauce)
1 large tomato (sauce)
50 grams capsicum, red (sauce)
1 stalk celery, chopped (sauce)
1/2 tsp cumin, ground (sauce)
2 tbsp tomato paste (sauce)
1 sprig coriander (sauce)
40 grams prawns

Procedure

1. Mix the marinade, add fish fillets and marinate 1 - 2 hours.
2. Blend the tomato, capsicum, celery and cumin.
3. Heat a large frying pan to medium and dry fry the Spanish onion until soft. Add blended sauce mixture, bring to a high simmer. Stir in tomato paste, coriander leaves and cumin. Season to taste.
4. Cover a tagine base (or porcelain casserole dish) with some of the sauce. Add the marinated fish and peeled, cooked prawns, then cover with remaining sauce.
5. If you have a tagine, place the plate on the stove at medium heat to start the cooking process, then transfer to a pre-heated oven (180 degrees C) for 25 - 30 mins.
6. If using a casserole dish, place the filled dish into the oven, pre-heated to 180 degrees C, and cook for 25 – 30 mins.

Servings: 1

Prep. Time:10 mins; Cook. Time: 30 mins; Total Time: 40 mins

Nutrition Facts

Nutrition (per serving): 234 calories, 2.8g total fat, 131.4mg cholesterol, 193.5mg sodium, 1323.9mg potassium, 23.2g carbohydrates, 6.2g fibre, 10.8g sugar, 31.1g protein.

Fish, Zucchini and Oregano Bake

1/2 tsp coconut oil
1 small brown onion, diced
50 grams sweet potato, peeled and cubed
1 medium zucchini, cubed
100 grams broccoli florets
50 grams eggplant, diced
120 grams tomatoes, canned, diced
1 sprig oregano leaves
150 grams whiting or bream fillets

Procedure

1. Heat a heavy-based saucepan over medium heat; brush with oil and sauté onions until golden.
2. Add sweet potato and cook for 3 mins, stirring regularly.
3. Add zucchini, broccoli, eggplant, tomatoes and half of the oregano. Bring to the boil.
4. Reduce heat to low, cover and cook for 8 - 10 mins or until sweet potato is tender. Stir in fish.
5. Simmer, uncovered, for 4 - 5 mins or until fish is cooked through.
6. Top with remaining oregano leaves and serve with a green salad.

Servings: 1

Preparation Time: 10 mins; Cooking Time: 15 mins; Total Time: 25 mins

Nutrition Facts

Nutrition (per serving): 321 calories, 5.6g total fat, 100.5mg cholesterol, 353.7mg sodium, 1829.6mg potassium, 35.9g carbohydrates, 7.7g fibre, 14.6g sugar, 35.9g protein.

Italian Chicken Salad

160 grams chicken breasts
1 tbsp balsamic vinegar
1 tsp mixed Italian herbs
2 cups lettuce, shredded
1/4 avocado, diced
20 grams snow peas, chopped in half
1 tbsp cashews, chopped
2 tbsp lemon juice
1 pinch black pepper
1 pinch Himalayan salt
1 tsp extra virgin olive oil

Procedure

1. Coat chicken in Italian herbs and balsamic, cook on barbecue or non-stick frypan, until cooked through.
2. Rest 5 mins, then slice chicken thinly.
3. Mix lettuce, avocado and snow peas and mix with cashew nuts.
4. Dress salad with chicken slices.
5. Mix lemon juice, 1 tsp oil, salt and pepper in a bowl, then drizzle over the salad.

Servings: 1

Preparation Time: 5 mins; Cooking Time: 15 mins; Total Time: 20 mins

Nutrition Facts

Nutrition (per serving): 407 calories, 21.3g total fat, 102.4mg cholesterol, 496.4mg sodium, 1164.1mg potassium, 17.8g carbohydrates, 6.5g fibre, 7.4g sugar, 38.1g protein.

Recipe Tip

Use leftover chicken and sweet potato to make this meal even quicker.

Mushroom Silverbeet Frittata

1/2 tsp coconut oil
1 whole Spanish onion, finely chopped
40 grams mushrooms, sliced
100 grams silverbeet (chard), raw, chopped
2 whole eggs, lightly beaten
2 egg whites, lightly beaten

Procedure

1. Heat a non-stick pan to medium heat and melt coconut oil.
2. Lightly sauté onions, then add mushrooms and stir until browned.
3. Add chopped silverbeet and stir to combine.
4. Pour beaten eggs and whites over the top and cook until set.

Servings: 1

Preparation Time: 5 mins; Cooking Time: 7 mins; Total Time: 12 mins

Nutrition Facts

Nutrition (per serving): 245 calories, 12.3g total fat, 372mg cholesterol, 469.5mg sodium, 753.1mg potassium, 10.8g carbohydrates, 3g fibre, 2.7g sugar, 23.5g protein.

Parmesan Bream with Asparagus

2 tbsp almond meal
1 tsp dried basil
2 tbsp parsley, finely chopped
1 tbsp parmesan cheese (or nutritional yeast)
1 whole egg
120 grams bream (or whiting) fillets
100 grams pumpkin, cubed
100 grams asparagus spears, fresh
1 tsp coconut oil

Procedure

1. Mix almond meal, fresh and dried herbs and parmesan with a fork.
2. In a separate bowl, lightly beat the egg.
3. Coat the fish in beaten egg then roll in crumb mix until evenly coated; refrigerate.
4. Cook the pumpkin cubes (steam or dry fry) for 5 mins, then add the asparagus and cook for about 5 mins or until tender.
5. Meanwhile, heat a pan and add the oil. Fry the fish on each side for 2 - 3 mins, or until golden.
6. Serve fish with pumpkin and asparagus, and a wedge of fresh lemon and cherry tomatoes if desired.

Servings: 1

Preparation Time: 5 mins; Cooking Time: 10 mins; Total Time: 15 mins

Nutrition Facts

Nutrition (per serving): 360 calories, 18.5g total fat, 270.8mg cholesterol, 242.3mg sodium, 1078.7mg potassium, 14.7g carbohydrates, 4.8g fibre, 5.4g sugar, 36.4g protein.

Peppered Lamb, Pea and Mint Salad

1 tsp peppercorns
150 grams lamb, lean steak
1/2 tsp coconut oil
1.5 tbsp white wine vinegar (vinaigrette)
1 clove garlic clove, crushed (vinaigrette)
1/2 tsp coconut oil (vinaigrette)
1 cup watercress leaves
3 tbsp mint leaves, chopped
75 grams snow peas, chopped in half
5 whole cherry tomatoes, halved

Procedure

1. Grind peppercorns with a mortar and pestle, or in a pepper grinder.
2. Combine peppercorns with lamb steak in a bowl. Cook lamb in a pre-heated frypan brushed with coconut oil and cook as desired.
3. Remove from heat, allow lamb to stand 5 mins, then slice thinly.
4. For vinaigrette, mix white wine vinegar with garlic, adding coconut oil if desired. Shake well.
5. Arrange salad ingredients in a bowl, place lamb over the top and drizzle with dressing.

Servings: 1

Preparation Time: 10 mins; Cooking Time: 10 mins; Total Time: 20 mins

Nutrition Facts

Nutrition (per serving): 409 calories, 20g total fat, 147mg cholesterol, 143.4mg sodium, 985.8mg potassium, 14.4g carbohydrates, 4g fibre, 3.1g sugar, 43g protein.

Prawn and Pink Grapefruit Salad

150 grams king prawns, peeled and de-veined

1 tbsp red wine vinegar

2 pinches stevia

20 grams mint, chopped

1 small chili pepper, finely chopped

1/2 tsp coconut oil (optional)

300 grams lettuce, cos, roughly torn

1 cup watercress leaves

80 grams pink grapefruit, segmented

Procedure

1. Shell and de-vein prawns; leave tails intact (if desired).
2. Make the chilli mint dressing by combining the vinegar, stevia, mint and chili (and coconut oil - optional).
3. Add lettuce, watercress, prawns and grapefruit to the serving plate and top with dressing.
4. Serve immediately.

Servings: 1

Preparation Time: 15 mins; Total Time: 15 mins

Nutrition Facts

Nutrition (per serving): 270 calories, 4.5g total fat, 241.5mg cholesterol, 227.9mg sodium, 1621.7mg potassium, 25.8g carbohydrates, 10g fibre, 11.5g sugar, 36.8g protein.

Acknowledgement

Image supplied by Anne Reid; www.bayremovals.com.au

Prawn Laksa

40 grams onion, chopped
1 tsp turmeric, ground or grated
1 small chili pepper
1 tsp lemongrass
1 tbsp curry paste
1 tsp ginger, minced
75 ml chicken stock, home made
100 ml coconut milk
125 ml cold water
1 serve Slim Pasta
1/2 cup bean sprouts
150 grams prawns
1 sprig coriander leaves (garnish)
1 tsp chili, chopped (garnish) optional
2 wedges lime

Procedure

1. Puree the onion and the first five herbs to form the laksa paste.
2. Heat a saucepan to medium, add the paste mix and stir for 2 mins until fragrant.
3. Add stock, coconut milk and 1/2 cup cold water, cover and bring to the boil.
4. Add 1 serve of slim pasta/konjac noodles and simmer for 4 mins until noodles are tender.
5. Add prawns, and simmer for 2 - 3 mins until prawns are pink.
6. Serve in a bowl, top with bean sprouts, fresh coriander and chilli, and with lime wedges on the side.

Servings: 1

Prep. Time:10 mins; Cook. Time: 15 mins; Total Time: 25 mins

Nutrition Facts

Nutrition (per serving): 378 calories, 15.9g total fat, 243.8mg cholesterol, 455.5mg sodium, 1017.2mg potassium, 25.5g carbohydrates, 4.1g fibre, 11.8g sugar, 37.6g protein.

Rosemary Salmon and Asparagus

130 grams salmon steak
1 tsp lemon juice
1 tsp olive oil
1 clove garlic, minced
1 tsp rosemary, fresh, chopped
1 pinch Himalayan salt
1 pinch pepper
75 grams asparagus spears, fresh
3 cups lettuce, mixed types, shredded

Procedure

1. Place salmon skin-side down on a piece of aluminium foil.
2. Coat fish with mixed lemon juice, olive oil, garlic, rosemary, salt and pepper.
3. Wrap and leave a small gap in foil for steam to escape. Place foil packet on barbecue grill and cook for 10 - 15 mins.
4. Meanwhile, grill asparagus spears directly on the grill for 5 mins, turning regularly to avoid burning.
5. Serve with a fresh mixed lettuce salad.

Servings: 1

Preparation Time: 10 mins; Cooking Time: 15 mins; Total Time: 25 mins

Nutrition Facts

Nutrition (per serving): 357 calories, 22.4g total fat, 71.5mg cholesterol, 386.4mg sodium, 888.7mg potassium, 9.8g carbohydrates, 3.9g fibre, 4.8g sugar, 30g protein.

San Choy Bau

1 small onion, finely diced
1 whole carrot, finely diced
1 small zucchini, finely diced
150 grams turkey mince, lean
2 tbsp tamari
1 tsp ginger, freshly grated
1/2 tsp sesame oil (or substitute)
1 pinch stevia
2 sprigs coriander, finely chopped
1 tsp sesame seeds (optional)
100 grams lettuce, cos, roughly torn

Procedure

1. Heat a non-stick pan and dry fry the mince.
2. Add the chopped veg, tamari, ginger, stevia and sesame (or other) oil, stir well and cook about 5 mins.
3. Turn off heat and add coriander leaves and sesame seeds (if using).
4. Stir well and serve mixture in lettuce cups.

Servings: 1

Preparation Time: 5 mins; Cooking Time: 15 mins; Total Time: 20 mins

Nutrition Facts

Nutrition (per serving): 379 calories, 16.2g total fat, 103.5mg cholesterol, 2172.2mg sodium, 1383.4mg potassium, 23.8g carbohydrates, 7.4g fibre, 11.3g sugar, 38.1g protein.

Sate Chicken

1/2 tsp coconut oil
120 grams chicken breast strips
1 tsp coriander, ground
1 tsp cumin, ground
1 pinch chilli flakes
1 clove garlic, minced
2 whole spring onions, chopped
1 tbsp peanut butter, 100% peanut
1 tbsp lime juice
2 tbsp Bragg's sauce or tamari
1 tbsp coconut milk or water
50 grams carrots, cut into sticks
4 stalks celery, cut into sticks
1 medium zucchini, cut into sticks
1 serve Grated Cauliflower (Rice)

Procedure

1. Heat oil in a pan over medium heat and cook chicken until browned and just cooked through.
2. Add the vegetables to the pan and stir fry until cooked through. Set chicken and vegetables aside.
3. In the same pan, add coriander, cumin, garlic, spring onions and chilli flakes and fry for about 30 seconds.
4. Add the peanut butter, chilli, lime juice, coconut milk (or water) and Bragg's sauce (or tamari).
5. Stir to form a paste and add extra water, gradually, until desired consistency is achieved.
6. Add chicken and vegetables to the sauce, stir to coat well.
7. Heat 2 mins. Serve with Grated Cauliflower (Rice) (page 78).

Servings: 1

Prep. Time: 5 mins; Cooking Time: 15 mins; Total Time: 20 mins

Nutrition Facts

Nutrition (per serving): 440 calories, 18.9g total fat, 76.8mg cholesterol, 2397.9mg sodium, 2255.9mg potassium, 32.9g carbs, 11.9g fibre, 15.5g sugar, 40.7g protein.

Sautéed Beef in Indian Spinach Sauce

1/2 brown onion, diced
1/2 tsp fresh ginger root
2 cloves garlic
1 tsp olive oil
120 grams sirloin steak, cubed
50 ml water
100 grams Greek yoghurt
1/2 tsp curry powder
1 pinch black pepper, ground
1 pinch Himalayan salt
100 grams spinach leaves
1 tsp garam masala

Procedure

1. Puree onion, ginger and garlic in a food processor.
2. Heat the olive oil in a large frypan, brown the puree and cook for about 10 mins until golden and reduced. Remove from pan and set aside.
3. Sautee the cubed sirloin for a few mins until brown.
4. Return puree to the pan and add the water.
5. Stir, then add yoghurt 1 tbsp at a time, stirring constantly.
6. Add curry powder, salt and pepper.
7. As the mixture bubbles, begin adding spinach. Cover and simmer 5 mins.
8. Remove from heat, stir through garam masala, and serve.

Servings: 1

Preparation Time: 10 mins; Cooking Time: 10 mins; Total Time: 20 mins

Nutrition Facts

Nutrition (per serving): 336 calories, 14.3g total fat, 64.8mg cholesterol, 492.6mg sodium, 702.1mg potassium, 19.3g carbohydrates, 3.9g fibre, 9.8g sugar, 35.1g protein.

Recipe Tips

Grated cauliflower rice is a delicious accompaniment to this dish.
Image supplied by Anne Reid of www.bayremovals.com.au

Savoury Baked Tofu

2 tsp lemon juice, freshly squeezed
2 tsp Dijon mustard
1 tsp thyme
1 clove garlic clove, crushed
120 grams tofu

Procedure

1. Preheat oven to 200 degrees C.
2. Mix herbs and garlic together with lemon juice.
3. Place tofu in a baking dish in a little water, enough to cover the bottom of the dish.
4. Pour herb mix over the tofu and bake for 30 - 40 mins until tender and golden.
5. Serve with salad or vegetables.

Servings: 1

Preparation Time: 10 mins; Cooking Time: 35 mins; Total Time: 45 mins

Nutrition Facts

Nutrition (per serving): 127 calories, 7.6g total fat, 0mg cholesterol, 136.2mg sodium, 205.3mg potassium, 5.6g carbohydrates, 1.4g fibre, <1g sugar, 12.7g protein.

Recipe Tips

To speed up cooking time, cut tofu into wedges.
Tempeh can be used instead of tofu in this recipe.

Shakshuka

30 grams onion, chopped

40 grams carrot, finely chopped

1 clove garlic, chopped

1 whole zucchini, cubed

100 grams tomato puree

1/2 tsp paprika

1 tsp oregano, chopped

2 tsp red wine vinegar

1 cup water

2 whole eggs

50 grams ricotta cheese, extra light

Procedure

1. Heat a non-stick pan to medium and dry fry carrot and onion until golden.
2. Add zucchini and garlic and stir fry for 5 mins.
3. Stir in tomato puree, oregano, vinegar, paprika and water. Season to taste.
4. Bring mixture to the boil, then reduce heat to low and simmer for 20 mins, stirring occasionally or until thickened.
5. Make four small indents in the mixture and break eggs into two, and spoon ricotta cheese into the other two.
6. Partially cover with foil or a lid and cook for 10 mins, or until eggs set.

Servings: 1

Preparation Time: 10 mins; Cooking Time: 20 mins; Total Time: 30 mins

Nutrition Facts

Nutrition (per serving): 311 calories, 14.6g total fat, 387.5mg cholesterol, 783.1mg sodium, 1295.1mg potassium, 23.6g carbohydrates, 6.1g fibre, 13.3g sugar, 23.2g protein.

Simple Tuna Salad

100 grams spinach leaves, stems removed and sliced into strips

3 whole celery stalks, chopped

1/2 small Spanish onion, finely chopped

1 whole artichoke heart, sliced

1/4 whole avocado, diced

185 grams tuna, capsicum and bean mix, canned

2 tbsp apple cider vinegar

Procedure

1. Mix salad ingredients together.
2. Stir through canned tuna, capsicum and bean mix.
3. Drizzle apple cider vinegar over the top and serve immediately.

Servings: 1

Preparation Time: 5 mins; Total Time: 5 mins

Nutrition Facts

Nutrition (per serving): 473 calories, 21.8g total fat, 0mg cholesterol, 1314.5mg sodium, 1191.4mg potassium, 39.1g carbohydrates, 19.9g fibre, 5.1g sugar, 31.9g protein.

Slim Singapore Noodle Tofu Stir Fry

1/2 tsp coconut oil
120 grams tofu, cubed (2cm)
1 whole egg
1 clove garlic, minced
1 whole chili pepper, finely chopped
1 whole Spanish onion, chopped
2 stalks celery, diced
1 cup Pakchoy, shredded
1 serve Slim Pasta
1 tbsp tamari
1 tsp fish sauce
1 pinch stevia
1 tsp ginger, freshly grated
1 whole spring onion, chopped

Procedure

1. Bring a small pot of water to the boil and add the egg, cook for 4 - 5 mins to hard boil. Set aside to cool, remove shell.
2. Heat the coconut oil in a non-stick pan and lightly fry the garlic and chili until fragrant; add tofu and brown evenly.
3. Add the onion and celery, stir fry for a few mins until tender.
4. Drain Slim Pasta, pour into separate bowl, top with boiling water to cover.
5. Add cabbage to frypan; toss through quickly (2 mins).
6. Mix tamari, fish sauce and stevia together; turn off the heat and stir the sauce through the pan ingredients.
7. Drain Slim Pasta and add to the pan, stirring quickly to mix.
8. Transfer to serving bowl, top with halved egg, ginger and spring onions.

Servings: 1

Preparation Time: 10 mins; Cooking Time: 10 mins; Total Time: 20 mins

Nutrition Facts

Nutrition (per serving): 286 calories, 14.7g total fat, 186mg cholesterol, 1683.6mg sodium, 901.6mg potassium, 19.2g carbohydrates, 4.9g fibre, 6.6g sugar, 24g protein.

Spaghetti Bolognaise

1 clove garlic, minced
30 grams onions, chopped
120 grams lean beef, minced
75 grams tomato paste
50 grams spinach leaves
1 sprig parsley, finely chopped
1 sprig oregano leaves, crushed
1 sprig basil, chopped
1 serve Slim Pasta
1/2 cup water (if desired)

Procedure

1. Heat a non-stick pan to medium heat.
2. Add the garlic and onions, sauté until lightly browned.
3. Add the beef mince and sauté until evenly browned.
4. Add tomato paste, and up to 1/2 cup of water to obtain a good consistency.
5. Add chopped fresh herbs and spinach in the last three mins of cooking.
6. Season with salt and pepper if desired.
7. Serve immediately with Slim Pasta.

Servings: 1

Preparation Time: 10 mins; Cooking Time: 15 mins; Total Time: 25 mins

Nutrition Facts

Nutrition (per serving): 263 calories, 6.6g total fat, 74.4mg cholesterol, 172.3mg sodium, 1534.1mg potassium, 20.7g carbohydrates, 9.7g fibre, 11.1g sugar, 31.1g protein.

Recipe Tips

Pour boiling water over the konjac noodles to heat through. Noodles can be softened by boiling lightly for 2 - 5 mins in a saucepan of water.

Spanish Salad with Grilled Pork

150 grams pork fillet
1 tsp paprika
1/2 small orange, chopped
1 small Spanish onion, finely chopped
60 grams red capsicum, slice
100 grams spinach leaves
1 serve Orange vinaigrette
6 pitted black olives, sliced
1 tsp pine nuts, toasted and chopped
1 sprig parsley, chopped

Procedure

1. Season the pork with paprika, and grill on the barbecue over medium heat. Sear the meat for 2 - 3 mins, then cook for a further 3 - 4 mins or until tender.
2. Cover and stand for a few mins, then slice.
3. Toss sliced pork with salad ingredients to combine.
4. Drizzle with dressing.
5. Garnish with olives, pine nuts and parsley.

Servings: 1

Preparation Time:10 mins; Cooking Time: 10 mins; Total Time: 20 mins

Nutrition Facts

Nutrition (per serving): 349 calories, 9.2g total fat, 97.5mg cholesterol, 398mg sodium, 1586.1mg potassium, 31g carbohydrates, 9.9g fibre, 5.9g sugar, 37.7g protein.

Recipe Tip

A delicious green salad works beautifully with this dish.

Spicy Zucchini and Capsicum Eggah

1 whole zucchini, thinly sliced
1 whole egg
2 egg whites (or one scoop plain protein powder)
1 tsp cumin seeds
1/2 tsp coriander seed, ground
1/2 tsp turmeric, ground or grated
1 pinch Himalayan salt
1 pinch black pepper
50 grams roasted capsicum
1 tsp coconut oil (or olive oil)

Procedure

1. Preheat the grill. Place sliced zucchini on a non-stick tray and grill on both sides until just golden and cooked through. Set aside.
2. Mix eggs (protein powder if using) and spices, salt, pepper.
3. Heat a non-stick pan and brush with oil.
4. Add the egg mix and swirl evenly to coat the bottom of the pan evenly.
5. Arrange the cooked zucchini and capsicum slices over the egg mix.
6. Cook for 2 - 3 mins in the pan, then transfer to hot grill to brown the eggs.
7. Remove from the grill and serve immediately with mixed salad.

Servings: 1

Preparation Time: 10 mins; Cooking Time: 10 mins; Total Time: 20 mins

Nutrition Facts

Nutrition (per serving): 211 calories, 10.9g total fat, 186mg cholesterol, 494.6mg sodium, 892.4mg potassium, 13.1g carbohydrates, 4.2g fibre, 5.9g sugar, 17.2g protein.

Stuffed Beef Capsicums

1 whole bell pepper
120 g beef mince
½ tsp coconut oil
1 clove garlic clove, crushed
1 sprig basil leaves, chopped
50 g broccoli florets
50 g mushrooms, sliced thin
50 g spinach leaves
50 g zucchini thinly sliced

Procedure

1. Heat oven to 180 degrees C.
2. Slice capsicum in half and set aside.
3. Fry beef mince on medium heat with coconut oil, garlic and basil.
4. Chop remaining ingredients into small cubes, mix well, stir through mince and basil mix. Add about 1 tablespoon of water to add moisture to the mix, or more if required to moisten.
5. Fill each capsicum half with the mince and vegetable mix.
6. Bake in a preheated oven for about 15 mins, or until golden.

Servings: 1

Preparation Time: 10 mins; Cooking Time: 15 mins; Total Time: 25 mins

Nutrition Facts

Nutrition (per serving): 274 calories, 9g total fat, 74.1mg cholesterol, 146mg sodium, 1516.2mg potassium, 18.6g carbohydrates, 5.7g fibre, 9.4g sugar, 32.6g protein.

Tamarind Chicken

2 tsp coconut oil
120 grams chicken breasts
1 tbsp lemongrass, minced
1 tsp ginger, minced
1 small chili pepper, finely chopped
1 tsp tamarind paste
1 tsp stevia
1 tbsp lime juice
75 grams broccolini
50 grams green beans
10 whole cherry tomatoes, halved
1 serve Slim Pasta or konjac noodles

Procedure

1. Heat half the oil in a wok on medium high heat. Add chicken and stir fry until browned; remove from heat and set aside.
2. Add remaining oil, lemongrass, ginger and chili to the pan. Cook for 1 minute or until aromatic.
3. Drain Slim Pasta and soak in boiling water for 2 mins.
4. Return chicken to the pan and add the tamarind, lime juice, stevia, beans, broccolini and tomatoes. Stir fry for 3 mins or until tender.
5. Toss noodles with other ingredients in the pan and serve to a plate.
6. Garnish with fresh chili or lime wedges.

Servings: 1

Preparation Time: 5 mins; Cooking Time: 20 mins; Total Time: 25 mins

Nutrition Facts

Nutrition (per serving): 339 calories, 13.3g total fat, 76.8mg cholesterol, 185.5mg sodium, 1439.3mg potassium, 28.3g carbohydrates, 4.5g fibre, 10.1g sugar, 31.3g protein.

Tamarind Tofu

2 tsp coconut oil
120 grams tofu, cubed (2cm)
1 tbsp lemongrass, minced
1 tsp ginger, minced
1 small chili pepper, finely chopped
1 tsp tamarind paste
1 tsp stevia
1 tbsp lime juice
75 grams broccolini
50 grams green beans
10 cherry tomatoes, halved
1 serve Slim Pasta

Procedure

1. Heat half the oil in a wok on medium high heat. Add tofu and stir fry until browned; remove from heat and set aside.
2. Add remaining oil, lemongrass, ginger and chili to the pan. Cook for 1 minute or until aromatic.
3. Drain Slim Pasta and soak in boiling water for 2 mins.
4. Return tofu to the pan and add the tamarind, lime juice, stevia, beans, broccolini and tomatoes. Stir fry for 3 mins or until tender.
5. Toss noodles with other ingredients in the pan and serve to a plate.
6. Garnish with fresh chili or lime wedges.

Servings: 1

Preparation Time: 5 mins; Cooking Time: 20 mins; Total Time: 25 mins

Nutrition Facts

Nutrition (per serving): 311 calories, 17.2g total fat, 0mg cholesterol, 55.9mg sodium, 1153.7mg potassium, 30.7g carbohydrates, 5g fibre, 10.7g sugar, 17.7g protein.

Tofu Ginger Curry with Beans and Capsicum

1 tsp coriander, ground
1 sprig basil leaves
1 clove garlic
1 stalk lemongrass
1 tsp cumin seeds
1 small chili pepper
1 tsp ginger root
1 tsp tamari
1 tsp lime juice
60 grams Spanish onion
20 ml coconut milk
100 grams tofu
1 leaf Kafir lime
2 sprigs coriander leaves (garnish
100 grams green beans
1 whole red capsicum, diced

Procedure

1. Make curry paste by processing or blending all herbs (except Kefir lime leaf and coriander garnish) with garlic, onion, ginger, tamari. Chilli is optional.
2. Add coconut milk and process again.
3. Heat a non-stick pan to medium and stir fry the paste until fragrant (about 1 min), then add tofu and stir to combine, cook chicken through.
4. Add lime leaves, reduce heat, cover and simmer for 5 mins.
5. Add red capsicum and beans, stir and cook for 2 - 3 mins, until beans are bright green. Increase saltiness with 1 tsp of tamari or decrease saltiness with a little fresh lime juice. Top with coriander.

Servings: 1

Preparation Time: 5 mins; Cooking Time: 20 mins; Total Time: 25 mins

Nutrition Facts

Nutrition (per serving): 237 calories, 11.4g total fat, 0mg cholesterol, 366.6mg sodium, 752.6mg potassium, 25.5g carbohydrates, 6.1g fibre, 6.5g sugar, 15.4g protein.

Tofu Stir Fry

1 tsp coriander seed, ground
1 clove garlic, chopped
1 tsp ginger, freshly grated
1 tsp tamari
1 tbsp lime juice
100 grams tofu, cubed (2cm)
100 grams cabbage, shredded
100 grams mushrooms, sliced
50 grams broccoli florets

Procedure

1. Combine herbs, tamari and lime juice, and mix well.
2. Toss cubed tofu through marinade and marinate for up to an hour.
3. Chop vegetables into slices.
4. Heat a non-stick pan on medium heat; remove tofu from marinade and add to pan, dry frying until crisp.
5. Add vegetables and stir quickly, then add leftover marinade and stir until the liquid thickens.
6. Serve immediately.

Servings: 1

Preparation Time:5 mins; Cooking Time: 10 mins; Inactive Time: 1 hour
Total Time: 1 hour and 15 mins

Nutrition Facts

Nutrition (per serving): 218 calories, 8.8g total fat, 0mg cholesterol, 738.4mg sodium, 846.3mg potassium, 24.4g carbohydrates, 6.2g fibre, 11.8g sugar, 15.4g protein.

Tofu Tagine

1 clove garlic clove, crushed (marinade)
2 tsp lemon juice (marinade)
1/2 tsp cumin, ground (marinade)
1 sprig coriander, finely chopped (marinade)
30 ml water (marinade)
100 grams tofu
1 whole Spanish onion, finely chopped (sauce)
1 large tomato (sauce)
50 grams capsicum, red (sauce)
1 stalk celery, chopped (sauce)
1/2 tsp cumin, ground (sauce)
2 tbsp tomato paste (sauce)
1 sprig coriander (sauce)

Procedure

1. Mix the marinade ingredients together and add tofu slice, marinate for 1 - 2 hours in the fridge.
2. Blend the tomato, capsicum, celery and cumin.
3. Heat a large frying pan to medium and dry fry the Spanish onion until soft. Add blended sauce mixture, bring to a high simmer. Stir in tomato paste, coriander leaves and cumin. Season.
4. Cover a tagine base (or casserole dish) with some of the sauce. Add marinated tofu, then cover with remaining sauce.
5. If you have a tagine, place the plate on the stove at medium heat to start the cooking process, then transfer to a pre-heated oven (180 degrees C) for 25 - 30 mins.
6. If using a casserole dish, simply place the filled dish into the oven, pre-heated to 180 degrees C, and cook for 25 - 30 mins.

Servings: 1

Preparation Time: 10 mins; Cooking Time: 30 mins; Inactive Time: 2 hours; Total Time: 2 hours and 40 mins

Nutrition Facts

Nutrition (per serving): 201 calories, 7.1g total fat, 0mg cholesterol, 81.9mg sodium, 1101.3mg potassium, 25.2g carbohydrates, 6.6g fibre, 11.3g sugar, 14.7g protein.

Turkey burgers

200 grams turkey mince, lean
20 grams feta cheese, crumbled
1 tsp oregano, dried
4 black olives, sliced

Procedure

1. Preheat the barbecue to medium high heat.
2. In a large bowl, combine all ingredients and mix well, shaping into three patties.
3. Lightly oil the grill and barbecue the patties for 10 - 12 mins, turning halfway through to cook evenly.
4. Serve with a large fresh salad.

Servings: 1
Yield: 3 patties

Preparation Time: 5 mins; Cooking Time: 10 mins; Total Time: 15 mins

Nutrition Facts

Nutrition (per serving): 373 calories, 21.5g total fat, 155.8mg cholesterol, 493mg sodium, 506.7mg potassium, 2.9g carbohydrates, 1.2g fibre, <1g sugar, 42.4g protein.

Zucchini Fettuccine

1 whole zucchini, unpeeled
30 grams onion, chopped
1 clove garlic, minced
140 grams turkey breast mince
200 grams tomatoes, canned, diced
2 tbsp tomato paste
2 sprigs basil leaves, chopped
2 sprigs oregano leaves, crushed

Procedure

1. Slice zucchini lengthways with a cheese or broad blade slicer to create long, thin strips. Cut in half lengthways if desired to make thinner strips.
2. Dry fry onion and garlic over moderate heat, then add mince and cook until browned.
3. Add tomatoes, tomato paste and herbs and cook on low heat for 10 mins.
4. Meanwhile, boil a saucepan of water and salt lightly. Add zucchini strips and cook for 1 - 2 mins to blanch the strips.
5. Drain zucchini and top with the sauce, serve immediately.

Servings: 1

Preparation Time: 15 mins; Cooking Time: 10 mins; Total Time: 25 mins

Nutrition Facts

Nutrition (per serving): 259 calories, 3.5g total fat, 60.2mg cholesterol, 1623.7mg sodium, 1745.1mg potassium, 30.4g carbohydrates, 6.8g fibre, 20.1g sugar, 30.1g protein.

Recipe Tip

Delicious served with a large green salad with olives and feta.

Zucchini, Haloumi and Herb Tarts

5 sprigs dill (fresh herb)
2 sprigs mint leaves
1 tbsp chives
150 grams ricotta cheese, light
1 whole egg
2 whole egg whites
1 pinch Himalayan salt
1 pinch black pepper, ground
1 medium zucchini, thinly sliced
1 tsp pumpkin seeds
30 grams Haloumi cheese, sliced
1/2 tsp coconut oil
1 tsp lemon juice
2 cups rocket

Procedure

1. Place a heavy-based tray in oven, preheat to 190 degrees C.
2. Roughly chop herbs. Remove 2 tbsp herbs and set aside.
3. Add ricotta, whole egg plus one white to the food processor, season with salt and pepper, process until just combined.
4. Thinly slice zucchinis, place in a bowl with pumpkin seeds (pepitas) and the remaining egg white. Toss to combine.
5. Cut Haloumi into 1cm pieces and set aside.
6. Brush a ramekin with coconut oil or line with baking paper.
7. Pour ricotta mixture into ramekin, top with zucchini mix then Haloumi cheese. Bake on preheated tray for 20 mins until set.
8. Sprinkle lemon juice over rocket and reserved herbs, toss.

Servings: 1

Prep. Time: 10 mins; Cook. Time: 20 mins; Total Time: 30 mins

Nutrition Facts

Nutrition (per serving): 414 calories, 18.4g total fat, 219.6mg cholesterol, 1206mg sodium, 1135.5mg potassium, 18.5g carbohydrates, 4.6g fibre, 11g sugar, 44.8g protein.

Notes

Note: this recipe is adapted from an original that uses filo pastry. There is no filo in this recipe.

5 Salad Dressings and Sauces

Coconut Lime Dressing

4 tbsp lime juice
4 tbsp coconut milk
2 pinch stevia
1 tsp coriander, finely chopped

Procedure

1 Mix all ingredients together and stir well.

Servings: 2

Preparation Time: 5 mins; Total Time: 5 mins

Nutrition Facts

Nutrition (per serving): 69 calories, 6.3g total fat, 0mg cholesterol, 5.1mg sodium, 116mg potassium, 4.3g carbohydrates, <1g fibre, <1g sugar, <1g protein.

Lemon Anchovy Dressing

2 small anchovy fillets
1 tbsp extra virgin olive oil
2 tbsp lemon juice, freshly squeezed
1 pinch black pepper
1 tbsp thyme (or basil)

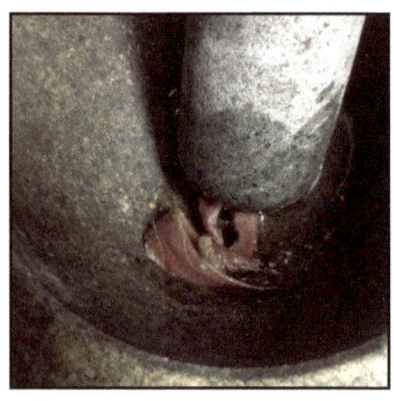

Procedure

1 Put all ingredients into a mortar and pestle, or small mixer.
2 Grind together (or process) until thoroughly mixed.

Servings: 2
Yield: 2 tbsp

Preparation Time: 10 mins; Total Time: 10 mins

Nutrition Facts

Nutrition (per serving): 73 calories, 7.2g total fat, 3.4mg cholesterol, 147.2mg sodium, 47.7mg potassium, 1.5g carbohydrates, <1g fibre, <1g sugar, 1.3g protein.

Recipe Tips

Try different fresh herbs for a different flavour.
This is not fishy tasting and should suit most palates.

Orange Vinaigrette

2 tbsp fresh orange juice
1 tbsp red wine vinegar
1 pinch stevia
1/2 tsp orange zest

Procedure

1 Mix all ingredients well before drizzling over your favourite salad.

Servings: 1

Preparation Time: 5 mins; Total Time: 5 mins

Nutrition Facts

Nutrition (per serving): 18 calories, <1g total fat, 0mg cholesterol, 1.5mg sodium, 69.9mg potassium, 3.5g carbohydrates, <1g fibre, 2.6g sugar, <1g protein.

Sumac and Orange Salad Dressing

1/2 tsp sumac
1 tbsp extra virgin olive oil
1 tbsp orange juice (fresh)
1 tbsp red wine vinegar

Procedure

1 Whisk all ingredients together, stirring well to mix sumac powder with the liquid. Serve with salad.

Servings: 4

Preparation Time: 5 mins; Total Time: 5 mins

Nutrition Facts

Nutrition (per serving): 34 calories, 3.4g total fat, 0mg cholesterol, 21.4mg sodium, 9.2mg potassium, <1g carbohydrates, <1g fibre, <1g sugar, <1g protein.

Vietnamese Coconut Dressing

1 whole chili pepper
1 sprig coriander
1 tbsp lime juice
1 tsp tahini
1 tbsp coconut milk
2 pinches stevia

Procedure

1 Whisk all ingredients together. Serve with salad.

Servings: 1

Preparation Time: 5 mins; Total Time: 5 mins

Nutrition Facts

Nutrition (per serving): 81 calories, 5.8g total fat, 0mg cholesterol, 11.9mg sodium, 237.4mg potassium, 7.1g carbohydrates, 1.3g fibre, 2.7g sugar, 2.2g protein.

6 Vegetables & salads – side dishes

Asian Coleslaw

150 grams pakchoy or savoy cabbage, shredded

100 grams cucumber peeled, seeded and cut into 1/4-inch cubes

50 grams red cabbage, shredded

2 spring onion

3 sprigs coriander

2 sprigs mint sprigs

1 tsp tamari

1 tsp apple cider vinegar

90 ml fresh orange juice

Procedure

1. Combine dressing ingredients (soy, orange juice, vinegar) in a cup and mix well. Add a little stevia to taste if desired.
2. Julienne the cucumber (thin sticks) and place in a bowl.
3. Finely shred the remaining ingredients and toss well.
4. Pour dressing over the salad and toss to combine.
5. Serve with your choice of grilled fish, chicken, beef or tofu.

Servings: 1

Preparation Time: 10 mins; Total Time: 10 mins

Nutrition Facts

Nutrition (per serving): 108 calories, <1g total fat, 0mg cholesterol, 457.2mg sodium, 968.7mg potassium, 23.2g carbohydrates, 4.3g fibre, 14.1g sugar, 5.6g protein.

Recipe Tips

Use organic apple cider vinegar.

Use an organic, naturally fermented soy sauce.

A wonderful side dish for fish, chicken or tofu.

Avocado, Spinach and Walnut Salad

1 tbsp walnuts, chopped
3 cups spinach leaves
1/4 medium avocado
20 grams feta cheese, crumbled
1 tsp lemon juice

Procedure

1. Toast walnut pieces in a non-stick pan for a few mins until golden.
2. Arrange spinach and avocado on a serving plate. Sprinkle over walnuts and crumbled feta.
3. Drizzle the salad with lemon juice; season to taste and serve.

Servings: 1

Preparation Time: 5 mins; Cooking Time: 5 mins; Total Time: 10 mins

Nutrition Facts

Nutrition (per serving): 204 calories, 16.9g total fat, 17.8mg cholesterol, 298mg sodium, 796.6mg potassium, 9.8g carbohydrates, 5.9g fibre, 1.9g sugar, 7.6g protein.

Recipe Tip

A side dish that is delicious with fish or lamb.

Carrot, Fennel and Apple Salad

2 whole fennel bulbs, shredded

3 medium carrots, purple and orange, grated

1 small apple, grated

2 sprigs mint leaves, chopped

1 sprig coriander leaves, roughly chopped

1 tbsp almonds, chopped and toasted

2 tbsp sumac and orange salad dressing

Procedure

1. Toss grated vegetables and chopped herbs together.
2. Top with toasted almonds and dressing.

Servings: 2

Preparation Time: 10 mins; Total Time: 10 mins

Nutrition Facts

Nutrition (per serving): 198 calories, 6.5g total fat, 0mg cholesterol, 208.3mg sodium, 1377.7mg potassium, 35g carbohydrates, 11.8g fibre, 10.4g sugar, 5g protein.

Recipe Tip

This recipe is delicious with crumbled goat's feta on top and served with tofu or chicken.

Cauliflower and Tomato Curry

150 grams cauliflower florets
2 cups boiling water (for blanching)
1 clove garlic clove, crushed
1 pinch chilli flakes
60 grams Spanish onion, finely chopped
1 large tomato, diced
3/4 cup water
1/4 tsp each cumin, coriander, cinnamon and turmeric
1 tbsp coriander leaves (garnish)

Procedure

1. Blanch cauliflower florets in boiling water for up to 1 minute.
2. Heat a non-stick pan to medium and add blanched florets, then stir fry for 4 - 5 mins until golden brown.
3. Add chopped onion and stir fry until translucent.
4. Add tomatoes and cook for 5 mins until heated and well mixed.
5. Cook covered on low heat for 3 mins.
6. Add 3/4 cup water and spices then cook until the mixture reaches a thick gravy consistency.
7. Garnish with chopped coriander leaves and serve with lean protein.

Servings: 1

Preparation Time: 5 mins; Cooking Time: 20 mins; Total Time: 25 mins

Nutrition Facts

Nutrition (per serving): 92 calories, 1g total fat, 0mg cholesterol, 87.2mg sodium, 830.7mg potassium, 19.1g carbohydrates, 6.1g fibre, 6.5g sugar, 5.2g protein.

Recipe Tip

This recipe works very well with beef, oily fish or tempeh.

Eggplant with Oregano and Lemon

1/2 medium eggplant, sliced lengthways (1cm thick)
1 clove garlic, minced
1 tsp extra virgin olive oil
1 tbsp oregano leaves, crushed
1 tbsp lemon juice, freshly squeezed

Procedure

1. Salt eggplant slices lightly, leave 5 mins.
2. Rinse well in fresh water and pat dry.
3. Mix the garlic, lemon juice and oil together.
4. Brush over the eggplant slices
5. Grill or bake until tender (~20 mins, medium heat), turning regularly.

Servings: 1
Yield: 3 slices

Preparation Time: 10 mins; Cooking Time: 20 mins; Total Time: 30 mins

Nutrition Facts

Nutrition (per serving): 128 calories, 5.2g total fat, 0mg cholesterol, 7.4mg sodium, 711.9mg potassium, 21.3g carbohydrates, 10.2g fibre, 10.3g sugar, 3.3g protein.

Recipe Tip

This recipe is delicious with lamb, oily fish or chicken.

Grated Cauliflower ('Rice')

100 grams cauliflower
1/2 tsp coconut oil

Procedure

1. Grate the cauliflower with a coarse-holed grater.
2. Heat a non-stick pan to medium and add coconut oil (if desired).
3. Add grated cauliflower and stir continuously until browned.

Servings: 1

Preparation Time: 5 mins; Cooking Time: 5 mins; Total Time: 10 mins

Nutrition Facts

Nutrition (per serving): 44 calories, 2.5g total fat, 0mg cholesterol, 30mg sodium, 299mg potassium, 5g carbohydrates, 2g fibre, 1.9g sugar, 1.9g protein.

Recipe Tips

Toss a handful of finely chopped fresh herbs or 1 tbsp dried herbs for a different flavour.

This dish is a perfect match with any curries, goulashes, hot pots, stir fries or casseroles.

Green Bean, Tomato and Lettuce Salad

70 grams green beans

2 whole tomatoes

3 cups lettuce, mixed types, shredded

1 sprig parsley, finely chopped

1 sprig basil, chopped

1 tsp balsamic vinegar or fresh lemon juice

Procedure

1 Toss all ingredients then top with vinegar or lemon juice.

Servings: 1

Preparation Time: 5 mins; Total Time: 5 mins

Nutrition Facts

Nutrition (per serving): 50 calories, <1g total fat, 0mg cholesterol, 13.5mg sodium, 468.2mg potassium, 10.8g carbohydrates, 3.5g fibre, 6.4g sugar, 2.5g protein.

Recipe Tip

This recipe is a great accompaniment for beef, fish, shellfish, tempeh, tofu, chicken, lamb or pork dishes.

Green Bean, Zucchini and Radish Stir Fry

70 grams green beans
70 grams zucchini, thinly sliced
50 grams radish, cut into strips
1 clove garlic
1/2 tsp rosemary, fresh, finely chopped

Procedure

1. Heat a non-stick pan to medium.
2. Dry fry the garlic briefly.
3. Add vegetables and toss briefly, then add rosemary and stir through.

Servings: 1

Preparation Time: 5 mins; Cooking Time: 10 mins; Total Time: 15 mins

Nutrition Facts

Nutrition (per serving): 47 calories, <1g total fat, 0mg cholesterol, 29.9mg sodium, 463.1mg potassium, 9.9g carbohydrates, 3.5g fibre, 5g sugar, 2.7g protein.

Recipe Tip

This recipe is a great accompaniment for beef, fish, tempeh, tofu, chicken, lamb or pork dishes.

Grilled Mushroom, Tomato and Basil Salad

3 large mushrooms, flat (approx. 75g each)

12 whole cherry tomatoes halved

1 clove garlic clove, chopped

2 tbsp balsamic vinegar

1 tsp coconut oil (optional)

3 sprigs basil leaves, chopped

Procedure

1. Combine mushrooms, tomato, half the vinegar and garlic in a bowl (add coconut oil if using).
2. Cook the mushroom mix on a heated grill plate on the barbecue, until mushrooms are browned lightly and heated through.
3. Arrange the mushroom mix on a plate, top with basil and drizzle with remaining balsamic vinegar.
4. Serve with a lean protein of your choice (see Recipe Tips).

Servings: 1

Preparation Time: 5 mins; Cooking Time: 5 mins; Total Time: 10 mins

Nutrition Facts

Nutrition (per serving): 166 calories, 5.9g total fat, 0mg cholesterol, 37.8mg sodium, 1239.7mg potassium, 23.4g carbohydrates, 4.6g fibre, 9.3g sugar, 9.2g protein.

Recipe Tip

Grilled beef or tofu is will be delicious with this dish; top your preferred protein source with oregano, basil and parsley dressing.

Mashed cauliflower and sweet potato

150 grams cauliflower florets
50 grams sweet potato, peeled and cubed
1 clove garlic
1 tsp coconut oil
1 tsp chives, finely chopped

Procedure

1. Steam cauliflower and sweet potato until tender (about 10 mins).
2. Heat a small non-stick pan and fry garlic in coconut oil until garlic is golden.
3. Add garlic to the steamed vegetables and mash well.
4. Season to taste before serving and top with chopped chives.

Servings: 1

Preparation Time: 5 mins; Cooking Time: 10 mins; Total Time: 15 mins

Nutrition Facts

Nutrition (per serving): 124 calories, 5g total fat, 0mg cholesterol, 73mg sodium, 632mg potassium, 18.6g carbohydrates, 4.6g fibre, 5g sugar, 3.9g protein.

Recipe Tips

Use a stick mixer to create a lovely texture.
This side dish goes nicely with red meats, goulash, lamb and/or fish.

Mediterranean Salad

1/4 whole avocado, diced
1 whole tomato, diced
1/2 whole zucchini, thinly sliced
50 grams cucumber, Lebanese with skin, diced
1 small red capsicum, diced
6 whole black olives, pitted and sliced
20 grams Haloumi cheese, sliced and grilled (optional)
1 tbsp apple cider vinegar (optional)
1/2 tsp lemon zest

Procedure

1. Grill zucchini and capsicum slices until tender.
2. Combine all ingredients, drizzle with vinegar (optional) and top with lemon zest.

Servings: 1

Preparation Time: 10 mins; Total Time: 10 mins

Nutrition Facts

Nutrition (per serving): 255 calories, 15.9g total fat, 18.4mg cholesterol, 289.9mg sodium, 990.1mg potassium, 21.3g carbohydrates, 8.4g fibre, 10.5g sugar, 9.7g protein.

Recipe Tip

This is delicious with chicken, pork or fish.

Mexican Salsa

1 sprig coriander, finely chopped

1 sprig parsley, finely chopped

1/2 tsp cumin, ground

1 tsp lemon juice

1 small Spanish onion, finely chopped

1 stalk celery, finely chopped

1 medium red bell pepper, seeded and diced

75 grams kale, finely chopped

75 grams cherry tomatoes, quartered

Procedure

1. Toss chopped vegetables and finely chopped herbs together.
2. Pour lemon juice over the top and toss to combine, serve immediately with your favourite protein source.

Servings: 1

Preparation Time: 5 mins; Total Time: 5 mins

Nutrition Facts

Nutrition (per serving): 122 calories, 1.7g total fat, 0mg cholesterol, 81.2mg sodium, 938.7mg potassium, 23.8g carbohydrates, 5.2g fibre, 6g sugar, 6.2g protein.

Recipe Tips

Refrigerate overnight for a more infused flavour.

This is a lovely accompaniment to pulled pork, beef or chicken, or with barbecued/grilled fish.

Middle Eastern Cauliflower

1 cup cauliflower florets
1 tsp cumin seeds
1 pinch Himalayan salt
1 small red onion, thinly sliced
1 tbsp slivered almonds, lightly toasted
1/4 cup mint leaves, chopped
1/4 cup parsley, flat-leaved, chopped
2 tbsp Greek yoghurt or labne (low-fat for Phase 2)

Procedure

1. Preheat oven to 180 degrees C.
2. Scatter cauliflower florets on a tray lined with baking paper.
3. Sprinkle with cumin and salt, bake 20 mins or until golden brown.
4. Remove florets from oven and toss with herbs, onion and almonds.
5. Spoon small dobs of yoghurt or labne onto the cauliflower and serve with a lean protein.

Servings: 1

Preparation Time: 10 mins; Cooking Time: 30 mins; Total Time: 40 mins

Nutrition Facts

Nutrition (per serving): 155 calories, 7.7g total fat, 0mg cholesterol, 358.4mg sodium, 517.5mg potassium, 17.6g carbohydrates, 5.1g fibre, 5.9g sugar, 7.7g protein.

Recipe Tip

Beautiful accompaniment to lean lamb roasts or chops.

Mushroom Stroganoff

1/2 whole onion, (small), finely diced

1 clove garlic, minced

1.5 cups mushrooms, quartered

1/2 tsp Herbamare vegetable stock powder

1/2 cup water

1 tsp tomato paste, no added salt

1/2 tsp black pepper freshly ground

1/2 tsp paprika, sweet

1 pinch Himalayan salt

1/2 cup milk (cow's, soy or almond)

Procedure

1. Dry fry onions and garlic over medium heat in a non-stick pan.
2. Add mushrooms and sauté until tender.
3. Add remaining ingredients, simmer for 10 mins until mushrooms are cooked and liquid absorbed.
4. Serve with your favourite lean protein source.

Servings: 1

Preparation Time: 10 mins; Cooking Time: 15 mins; Total Time: 25 mins

Nutrition Facts

Nutrition (per serving): 121 calories, 3.1g total fat, 9.8mg cholesterol, 2540.3mg sodium, 772.8mg potassium, 17.6g carbohydrates, 3g fibre, 11.8g sugar, 8.8g protein.

Recipe Tip

Delicious served with a side salad and a lean protein like tofu, fish or chicken.

Red Cabbage, Celery and Bokchoy Stir Fry

1 clove garlic

100 grams red cabbage, shredded

3 stalks celery, cut into sticks

100 grams cabbage, Asian (bokchoy, pakchoy), shredded

1/2 tsp fresh Thai basil, coarsely chopped

1 whole apple, cored and chopped

Procedure

1. Heat a non-stick pan to medium.
2. Dry fry the garlic briefly.
3. Turn off heat and add remaining vegetables, toss briefly, then add basil and stir through.

Servings: 1

Preparation Time: 5 mins; Cooking Time: 10 mins; Total Time: 15 mins

Nutrition Facts

Nutrition (per serving): 142 calories, <1g total fat, 0mg cholesterol, 180.9mg sodium, 977.6mg potassium, 33.2g carbohydrates, 9.3g fibre, 21.3g sugar, 4.9g protein.

Recipe Tip

A great side dish to accompany steak, chicken, tofu or fish.

Ricotta Salad

1 whole carrot, cut into rounds
30 grams kale, torn
100 grams spinach leaves
2 sprigs basil leaves, chopped
100 grams cucumber, thinly sliced
6 halves semi-dried tomatoes
150 grams ricotta, extra light
1 tbsp almonds, chopped
1 tsp lemon juice
1 tsp olive oil
1 pinch black pepper freshly ground, to taste
1 pinch Himalayan salt

Procedure

1. Toss chopped vegetables in a bowl.
2. Top with ricotta cheese and almonds.
3. Mix lemon juice with olive oil and spoon over the salad.
4. Season with salt and pepper (optional), serve immediately.

Servings: 1

Preparation Time: 5 mins; Total Time: 5 mins

Nutrition Facts

Nutrition (per serving): 307 calories, 10.9g total fat, 6mg cholesterol, 1315mg sodium, 1429.4mg potassium, 29.5g carbohydrates, 8.9g fibre, 14.3g sugar, 28.4g protein.

Recipe Tip

Delicious with some tuna or salmon, grilled kangaroo steaks or cooked chicken breast.

Roasted Sweet Potato with Macadamias

20 grams macadamia nuts

75 grams sweet potato, peeled and cubed

1/2 tsp coconut oil

1 pinch Himalayan salt

1 pinch black pepper freshly ground, to taste

1 tbsp parsley, chopped

Procedure

1. Brush sweet potato cubes (1cm cubes) with coconut oil and arrange on baking paper on an oven tray.
2. Add macadamia halves.
3. Bake at 180 degrees C until golden brown and cooked through.
4. Remove from oven and season with salt and pepper, toss through chopped parsley and serve.

Servings: 1

Preparation Time: 5 mins; Cooking Time: 20 mins; Total Time: 25 mins

Nutrition Facts

Nutrition (per serving): 231 calories, 17.5g total fat, 0mg cholesterol, 335.2mg sodium, 358.1mg potassium, 18.6g carbohydrates, 4.3g fibre, 4.1g sugar, 3g protein.

Recipe Tip

A hearty side dish to accompany lean pork steak, chicken, fish or tofu.

Semi-roasted Veg with Salsa Verde

50 grams broccoli florets
2 stalks celery, chopped
50 grams red bell pepper seeded and chopped
30 grams onion, chopped
1 sprig parsley, chopped
1 sprig basil, chopped
1 sprig mint, chopped
1 clove garlic clove, crushed

Procedure

1. Preheat oven to 180 degrees C.
2. Place vegetables on a non-stick tray (or on baking paper) and roast until just cooked but firm (20 - 30 mins).
3. When vegetables are cooked, toss with chopped herbs and season with salt and pepper.
4. Serve immediately with your favourite lean protein (see Recipe Tip).

Servings: 1

Preparation Time: 10 mins; Inactive Time: 30 mins; Total Time: 40 mins

Nutrition Facts

Nutrition (per serving): 64 calories, <1g total fat, 0mg cholesterol, 90.9mg sodium, 589.7mg potassium, 12.7g carbohydrates, 3.4g fibre, 5.1g sugar, 3.4g protein.

Recipe Tip

Delicious served with tofu, chicken, kangaroo, beef or lamb.

Steamed Italian Veg

100 grams spinach leaves
100 grams broccoli florets
100 grams cauliflower florets
100 grams green beans
1 tsp pine nuts
1 tsp oregano, chopped
1 tsp olive oil, extra virgin

Procedure

1. Steam the vegetables for 2 - 4 mins until bright, tender but still firm.
2. Remove from heat and toss with pine nuts, oregano and olive oil.
3. Serve as a side dish to a lean protein source (see Recipe Tip).

Servings: 1

Preparation Time: 5 mins; Cooking Time: 5 mins; Total Time: 10 mins

Nutrition Facts

Nutrition (per serving): 167 calories, 7.7g total fat, 0mg cholesterol, 142.2mg sodium, 1418.5mg potassium, 21.4g carbohydrates, 7.4g fibre, 5.7g sugar, 10g protein.

Recipe Tip

A simple side dish that works well with light fish, tofu or chicken.

Streaky Spinach Salad

1 sprig parsley, chopped
1 sprig basil leaves, chopped
150 grams spinach leaves
1/4 whole avocado, diced
4 black olives, sliced
50 grams asparagus spears, large, fresh
1 whole eggs, boiled
2 whole egg whites, boiled
1 rasher lean shoulder bacon, grilled (optional – not in Phase 3)

Procedure

1. Toss salad vegetables together.
2. Top with boiled egg, boiled egg white and chopped, cooked bacon (if using).

Servings: 1

Preparation Time: 7 mins; Cooking Time: 5 mins; Total Time: 12 mins

Nutrition Facts

Nutrition (per serving): 263 calories, 15.5g total fat, 212.6mg cholesterol, 465.4mg sodium, 1355.2mg potassium, 13.5g carbohydrates, 7.9g fibre, 2.8g sugar, 21.1g protein.

Recipe Tip

Delicious with lean lamb, pork or chicken.

Warm Summer Sumac Salad

1 small red capsicum, cut lengthways into 1" strips

1 small zucchini, cut lengthways into 1/4" strips

1 small eggplant, peeled and cut lengthways into 1/4" slices

1 small Spanish onion, sliced into wedges

1/2 tsp olive oil

1 tsp lemon juice

1 tsp sumac

1/2 small cucumber, Lebanese with skin, diced

4 green olives, sliced

1 tsp lemon zest

Procedure

1. Heat the barbecue plate to medium. Toss the sliced capsicum, zucchini, eggplant strips and onion wedges with the olive oil.
2. Grill for 10 - 15 mins, turning regularly, until soft and cooked through.
3. Remove the skins from the capsicums and add to other vegetables.
4. Mix lemon juice and sumac; drizzle over vegetables; toss well.
5. Add the cucumber and olives and toss again.
6. Top with lemon zest and serve with your preferred lean protein.

Servings: 1

Preparation Time: 5 mins; Cooking Time: 20 mins; Total Time: 25 mins

Nutrition Facts

Nutrition (per serving): 353 calories, 15.9g total fat, 0mg cholesterol, 1020.7mg sodium, 1751.7mg potassium, 52.8g carbohydrates, 22g fibre, 25g sugar, 9.1g protein.

Recipe Tip

Lovely accompaniment to lean lamb, pork, kangaroo, beef steak, oily fish or tempeh.

Zucchini Fritters

1 small red onion, diced
1 medium zucchini, unpeeled, and grated
1 small carrot, grated
1 whole egg, separated
1 egg white
1 tbsp almond meal
1 tsp toasted cumin seeds
1 pinch Himalayan salt
1/2 tsp lemon zest (optional)
1/2 tsp coconut oil

Procedure

1. Dry fry the onion until lightly browned.
2. Whisk the egg whites until stiff peaks form. Set aside.
3. Mix the onion with remaining ingredients and egg yolk.
4. Gently stir egg whites through the fritter mix.
5. Heat oil in a large non-stick pan over medium heat, spoon batter into pan.
6. Cook fritters for 2 - 3 mins each side, or until golden.
7. Serve with a large green salad.

Servings: 1
Yield: 4 fritters

Preparation Time: 10 mins; Cooking Time: 20 mins; Total Time: 30 mins

Nutrition Facts

Nutrition (per serving): 227 calories, 11.3g total fat, 186mg cholesterol, 473.4mg sodium, 903mg potassium, 18.8g carbohydrates, 5.5g fibre, 8.3g sugar, 15.1g protein.

Recipe Tip

Delicious with grilled fish, pork and/or Mashed Cauliflower and Sweet Potato (page 82).

Zucchini, Fennel and Mint Salad

1 medium zucchini, grated
1 whole fennel bulb, shredded
1 sprig mint leaves, chopped
1 tbsp Lemon Anchovy Dressing

Procedure

1. Combine vegetables and mint in a bowl.
2. A special zucchini grater can be used to make spaghetti-like ribbons.
3. Top with dressing and serve.

Servings: 1

Preparation Time: 10 mins; Total Time: 10 mins

Nutrition Facts

Nutrition (per serving): 181 calories, 8.3g total fat, 3.4mg cholesterol, 285.5mg sodium, 1546.3mg potassium, 25.2g carbohydrates, 9.7g fibre, 5.3g sugar, 6.7g protein.

Recipe Tip

Delicious accompaniment to beef, kangaroo, fish, tofu, tempeh, chicken or pork.

7 Snacks

Baked Chilli Ricotta

150 grams ricotta cheese, extra light
1 egg white
1 sprig chives, finely chopped
1 whole chili pepper, finely chopped

Procedure

1. Preheat oven to 180 degrees C and brush a one-cup ramekin dish with a little coconut oil (or spray oil).
2. Combine all ingredients and mix well. Season with salt and pepper (optional).
3. Spoon mixture into ramekin and smooth the surface.
4. Bake for 25 mins or until golden and set.
5. Serve immediately.

Servings: 1

Preparation Time: 5 mins; Cooking Time: 25 mins; Total Time: 30 mins

Nutrition Facts

Nutrition (per serving): 226 calories, 12g total fat, 46.5mg cholesterol, 243.1mg sodium, 258.6mg potassium, 8.2g carbohydrates, <1g fibre, <1g sugar, 20.9g protein.

Guacamole

1/2 whole avocado, mashed
1/2 whole tomato, diced
1/4 whole Spanish onion, very finely chopped
1 sprig coriander leaves, roughly chopped
1 pinch Himalayan salt
1/2 tsp Tabasco sauce
1/2 tsp lemon juice
3 stalks celery
1/2 cup green beans, blanched and refreshed in cold water

Procedure

1. Mash all ingredients except celery and beans until smooth and creamy.
2. Serve with celery sticks and fresh green beans.

Servings: 1

Preparation Time: 10 mins; Total Time: 10 mins

Nutrition Facts

Nutrition (per serving): 212 calories, 15.2g total fat, 0mg cholesterol, 427.7mg sodium, 1054.5mg potassium, 19.1g carbohydrates, 11.1g fibre, 5.8g sugar, 4.5g protein.

Roast Capsicum Dip with Green Beans

100 grams capsicum, red
1 clove garlic
1 sprig basil leaves
1 whole spring onion
1 pinch cayenne
1 pinch Himalayan salt
50 grams green beans

Procedure

1. Preheat grill to high and roast the capsicum with skin closest to the heat, for about 7 mins or until charred.
2. Hold with tongs and rinse quickly under cold water before peeling off the charred skin.
3. Place capsicum and other ingredients, except beans, into a food processor and blend until a rough puree forms.
4. Transfer dip to a serving bowl and serve with fresh beans.

Servings: 1

Preparation Time: 10 mins; Cooking Time: 10 mins; Total Time: 20 mins

Nutrition Facts

Nutrition (per serving): 71 calories, <1g total fat, 0mg cholesterol, 302.6mg sodium, 477mg potassium, 14.5g carbohydrates, 4.9g fibre, 8.1g sugar, 2.9g protein.

Recipe Tip

Blanching the beans quickly in hot water will bring out a beautiful green colour.

Cottage Cheese Snack

100 grams cottage cheese, low fat

1 tbsp chia seeds, pre-soaked

1 pinch stevia

1/2 cup blueberries

Procedure

1. Use chia seeds that have been soaked at least one hour in 5 tbsp water, to form a gel.
2. Combine cheese, chia and stevia and mix well.
3. Top with blueberries; serve immediately.

Servings: 1

Preparation Time: 5 mins; Inactive Time: 1 hour; Total Time: 1 hour and 5 mins

Nutrition Facts

Nutrition (per serving): 176 calories, 5.8g total fat, 10mg cholesterol, 332.3mg sodium, 180.5mg potassium, 18.4g carbohydrates, 5.2g fibre, 10.9g sugar, 14g protein.

Recipe Tip

Chia gel can be kept in a sealed container in the fridge for up to one week. Mix 1-part chia to 5 - 10 parts liquid.

Lemon Passionfruit Meringue Pie

1/4 cup almond meal
1 tsp coconut oil
1 pinch stevia
6 tbsp lemon juice
1 tbsp lemon zest
2 whole eggs, separated
1 egg white
1 passionfruit pulp and juice
1/2 tsp stevia (or to taste)
1/2 tsp vanilla extract
1 pinch cream of tartar

Procedure

1. Preheat oven to 180 degrees C. Blend almond meal, pinch stevia and coconut oil into a firm crumb mix.
2. Press into a ramekin lined with baking paper, to 1/2 cm thick.
3. Bake 12 - 15 mins, then turn oven down to 150 degrees C.
4. Simmer lemon juice, zest and remaining stevia in a saucepan for 2 mins.
5. Remove mix from the heat, slowly add egg yolks, stir vigorously until thick, and add passionfruit (return to heat if required).
6. Allow to cool and pour over base.
7. Whisk egg whites, stevia, cream of tartar and vanilla in a clean glass bowl until mix is glossy (not stiff).
8. Spoon egg whites over lemon mix, bake 15 mins at 150 degrees C, then 18 - 20 mins at 120 degrees C for another 18 - 20 mins.
9. Turn oven off and leave pie inside to cool.

Servings: 2
Yield: 1 small pie

Preparation Time: 10 mins; Cooking Time: 30 mins; Total Time: 40 mins

Nutrition Facts

Nutrition (per serving): 225 calories, 16.1g total fat, 186mg cholesterol, 101mg sodium, 346.4mg potassium, 10.1g carbohydrates, 2.4g fibre, 4.6g sugar, 12g protein.

Sweet Potato Truffles

1 cup sweet potatoes, peeled and cubed
2 tsp coconut oil
2 tbsp coconut milk
1 tbsp almond meal
1/2 tsp stevia
1/2 tsp vanilla extract
1 pinch salt
1 pinch nutmeg

Procedure

1. Steam sweet potato until tender, then drain well; mash and allow to cool. Drain any excess water.
2. Add coconut oil, milk and almond meal; mix well.
3. Add remaining ingredients and mix with hands.
4. Shape into small balls and refrigerate 30 mins before serving.

Servings: 8
Yield: 16 balls

Preparation Time: 5 mins; Cooking Time: 20 mins; Inactive Time: 30 mins; Total Time: 55 mins

Nutrition Facts

Nutrition (per serving): 37 calories, 2.3g total fat, 0mg cholesterol, 46mg sodium, 70.5mg potassium, 3.8g carbohydrates, <1g fibre, <1g sugar, <1g protein.

Recipe Tip

Add extra almond meal or coconut flour if mixture is too wet.

8 Desserts

Apple Snow

1 whole apple, cored and chopped
2 egg whites
1 tsp gelatine
1/2 tsp stevia
1/4 cup coconut milk
1/2 cup water

Procedure

1. Roughly chop the apple, place in a saucepan with 1/2 cup coconut milk and simmer with the lid on until the apple is soft.
2. Dissolve gelatine in 1/4 cup hot water, stir until gelatine is dissolved, and add to the saucepan.
3. Place in refrigerator until half set (30 - 60 mins).
4. Whip the egg white until stiff peaks form; add the stevia and whip to combine. If required, add a pinch of cream of tartar to the egg white to stiffen. Stir whipped egg white through the half-set gelatine. Refrigerate until firm.
5. Serve garnished with mint leaves and a sprinkle of cinnamon.

Servings: 1

Preparation Time: 10 mins; Cooking Time: 10 mins; Inactive Time: 1 hour; Total Time: 1 hour and 20 mins

Nutrition Facts

Nutrition (per serving): 326 calories, 12.4g total fat, 0mg cholesterol, 255.1mg sodium, 384mg potassium, 46.8g carbohydrates, 3.3g fibre, 39.2g sugar, 11g protein.

Acknowledgement

Chapter cover image and recipe image supplied by Belinda McDonald, www.myhealingkitchen.co.nz

Apple Snow, Low Fat

1 whole apple, cored and chopped
2 egg whites
1 tsp gelatine
1/2 tsp stevia
1/2 cup water

Procedure

1. Roughly chop the apple, place in a saucepan with 1/2 cup water and simmer with the lid on until the apple is soft.
2. Stir in the gelatine; add another 1/2 cup water if required, stir until gelatine is dissolved.
3. Place in refrigerator until half set (30 - 60 mins).
4. Whip the egg white to form stiff peaks; stir through stevia and cream of tartar, then the half-set gelatine. Refrigerate until firm.
5. Serve garnished with mint leaves and a sprinkle of cinnamon.

Servings: 1

Preparation Time: 10 mins; Cooking Time: 10 mins; Inactive Time: 1 hour; Total Time: 1 hour and 20 mins

Nutrition Facts

Nutrition (per serving): 214 calories, <1g total fat, 0mg cholesterol, 247.7mg sodium, 259.7mg potassium, 45.2g carbohydrates, 3.3g fibre, 39.2g sugar, 9.9g protein.

Acknowledgement

Image supplied by Belinda McDonald, www.myhealingkitchen.co.nz

Baked Apple

1 green apple, core removed
1/2 tsp vanilla extract
1/2 cup water
1/2 tsp cinnamon
1 pinch stevia (if desired, to taste)

Procedure

1. Preheat the oven to 180 degrees C.
2. Run a knife around the centre of the apple to score the skin.
3. Place the apple in a small baking dish.
4. Combine vanilla and water (and stevia if using) and pour into the centre of the apple.
5. Place in the oven and cook until tender, about 30 - 40 mins.
6. Remove and sprinkle with cinnamon; serve immediately.

Servings: 1

Preparation Time: 5 mins; Cooking Time: 45 mins; Total Time: 50 mins

Nutrition Facts

Nutrition (per serving): 129 calories, <1g total fat, 0mg cholesterol, 6.2mg sodium, 256.4mg potassium, 33.1g carbohydrates, 6.2g fibre, 24.2g sugar, <1g protein.

Acknowledgement

Image supplied by Belinda McDonald, www.myhealingkitchen.co.nz

Chocolate Ice Blocks

1 large avocado
1 tbsp cacao powder
1/2 tsp vanilla extract
1 pinch stevia (or to taste)

Procedure

1. Blend all ingredients with a stick mixer, or in a food processor.
2. Spoon into ice block moulds, then tap the moulds well to remove air bubbles.
3. Replace the sticks in the mould, transfer to the freezer.
4. Freeze for at least 3 hours and enjoy!

Servings: 2
Yield: 2 ice blocks

Preparation Time: 5 mins; Inactive Time: 2 hours; Total Time: 2 hours and 5 mins

Nutrition Facts

Nutrition (per serving): 152 calories, 13.6g total fat, 0mg cholesterol, 7.4mg sodium, 440.1mg potassium, 7.9g carbohydrates, 6.5g fibre, <1g sugar, 2.2g protein.

Chocolate (Avocado) Mousse

1 large avocado
1 tsp coconut oil
2 tbsp dark cacao powder (optional)
1 pinch stevia (or to taste)
1/2 cup raspberries
1 tsp flaked or shredded coconut (optional)

Procedure

1. Blend the avocado, cacao powder (if using) and stevia until thoroughly combined and creamy.
2. Add the coconut oil (this makes a firmer mousse).
3. Refrigerate until cold.
4. Toast coconut in a non-stick pan for 2 - 3 mins, until browned (if using).
5. Serve with fresh raspberries and flaked coconut (if using).

Servings: 2

Preparation Time: 5 mins; Inactive Time: 45 mins; Total Time: 50 mins

Nutrition Facts

Nutrition (per serving): 210 calories, 17.9g total fat, 0mg cholesterol, 10.7mg sodium, 537.1mg potassium, 13.4g carbohydrates, 10.1g fibre, 2.4g sugar, 3.5g protein.

Lemon Slice

1 cup almond meal
1 tbsp coconut oil
7 tbsp lemon juice
1 tbsp lemon zest
1/2 tsp stevia (or to taste)
2 whole eggs, lightly beaten
1/2 cup blueberries

Procedure

1. Preheat oven to 175 degrees C, line a tray with baking paper.
2. Blend almond meal, 1 tbsp lemon juice and coconut oil into a firm mix.
3. Press flat onto the tray, about 1/2 cm thick, and bake 12 - 15 mins.
4. Simmer 6 tbsp lemon juice with zest and stevia for 2 mins.
5. Remove from the heat, slowly add eggs, stir vigorously until thick.
6. Allow to cool and pour over base, scatter with blueberries.
7. Refrigerate at least 30 mins then slice into four pieces.

Servings: 4

Preparation Time: 10 mins; Cooking Time: 15 mins; Total Time: 25 mins

Nutrition Facts

Nutrition (per serving): 199 calories, 15.4g total fat, 93mg cholesterol, 36.3mg sodium, 245.8mg potassium, 10g carbohydrates, 3.6g fibre, 3.6g sugar, 8.4g protein.

Ricotta Apple Dream

15 grams whey protein
150 grams ricotta cheese, extra light
1 pinch stevia
1 whole apple, grated or stewed

Procedure

1. Stir whey protein and stevia into ricotta cheese.
2. Add grated or stewed apple and stir through.
3. Serve immediately, with a dusting of cinnamon or grated lemon rind (optional).

Servings: 1

Preparation Time: 5 mins; Total Time: 5 mins

Nutrition Facts

Nutrition (per serving): 338 calories, 13.9g total fat, 48mg cholesterol, 226.4mg sodium, 461.2mg potassium, 30.1g carbohydrates, 3.6g fibre, 15.4g sugar, 24.9g protein.

Strawberry Mousse

1 tsp gelatine
20 ml boiling water
1 large egg white
100 grams strawberries, sliced
1 tsp stevia
100 grams Greek yoghurt (or substitute soy yoghurt; low fat or full fat)

Procedure

1. Dissolve gelatin in boiling water.
2. In a separate bowl, beat egg white until stiff peaks form.
3. Gradually add stevia, beating well after each addition, then beat in strawberries.
4. Fold through gelatine mixture and yoghurt.
5. Pour into a serving glass and refrigerate until firm.
6. Garnish with extra strawberries.

Servings: 1

Preparation Time: 10 mins; Inactive Time: 1 hour; Total Time: 1 hour and 10 mins

Nutrition Facts

Nutrition (per serving): 239 calories, 4.7g total fat, 0mg cholesterol, 233mg sodium, 209.6mg potassium, 40.3g carbohydrates, 2g fibre, 36.2g sugar, 11.1g protein.

Recipe Tip

Replace Greek yoghurt with soy yoghurt if you are avoiding dairy.

Index

A

Apple Snow 104
Apple Snow, Low Fat.... 105
Asian Chicken Broth 14
Asian Coleslaw 73
Asparagus and Leek
Quiche............................ 23
Avocado, Spinach and
Walnut Salad 74

B

Baked Apple 106
Baked Chilli Ricotta.......... 97
Baked Quark 6
Balsamic Chicken 24
Beef Goulash 25
Berry Ricotta 7

C

Cajun Spiced Beef and
Garlicky Bean Salad 26
Carrot, Apple and Celery
Juice 2
Carrot, Fennel and Apple
Salad 75
Cauliflower and Tomato
Curry 76
Chargrilled Chicken with
Asian Coleslaw 27
Chargrilled Moroccan Lamb
.... 28
Chicken and Green Veg
Soup 15
Chicken and Mushroom
Casserole 29
Chicken and Pea Salad .. 30
Chicken and Raspberry
Salad 31
Chicken Cacciatore 32
Chicken Ginger Curry with
Green Beans and Capsicum
.... 33
Chicken Mediterranean... 34
Chicken Miso Soup 16

Chicken, Green Bean and
Broccoli Soup 17
Chilli Lime Chicken Salad 35
Chocolate Ice blocks 107
Chocolate Mousse 108
Coconut Lime Dressing... 67
Cottage Cheese Snack . 100
Crab and Apple Salad 36

D

Detox Juice 3

E

Eggplant Goulash 37
Eggplant with Oregano and
Lemon 77

F

Fish and Prawn Tagine ... 38
Fish, Zucchini and Oregano
Bake 39

G

Grated Cauliflower ('Rice')
.... 78
Green Autumn Soup 18
Green Bean, Tomato and
Lettuce Salad 79
Green Bean, Zucchini and
Radish Stir Fry 80
Green Berry Smoothie 8
Grilled Mushroom, Tomato
and Basil Salad 81
Guacamole 98

I

Italian Chicken Salad 40

L

Lamb Immune Booster
Soup 19
Lemon Anchovy Dressing 68
Lemon Passionfruit
Meringue Pie 101
Lemon Slice 109

M

Mashed cauliflower and sweet potato 82
Mediterranean Salad 83
Mediterranean Vegetable Frittata 9
Mexican Salsa 84
Middle Eastern Cauliflower 85
Mushroom Silverbeet Frittata 41
Mushroom Stroganoff 86

O

Omelette 10
Orange Vinegarette 69

P

Parmesan Bream with Asparagus 42
Peppered Lamb, Pea and Mint Salad 43
Prawn and Pink Grapefruit Salad 44
Prawn Laksa 45

R

Raw Creamed Fennel Soup 20
Red Cabbage, Celery and Bok Choy Stir Fry 87
Refreshing Juice 4
Ricotta Apple Dream 110
Ricotta Salad 88
Roast Capsicum Dip with Green Beans 99
Roasted Sweet Potato with Macadamias 89
Rosemary Salmon and Asparagus 46

S

San Choy Bau 47
Sate Chicken 48
Sauteed Beef in Indian Spinach Sauce 49
Savoury Baked Tofu 50

Scrambled Breakfast 11
Semi-roasted Veg with Salsa Verde 90
Shakshuka 51
Simple Tuna Salad 52
Slim Singapore Noodle Tofu Stir Fry 53
Spaghetti Bolognaise 54
Spanish Salad with Grilled Pork 55
Spicy Zucchini and Capsicum Eggah 56
Steamed Veg 91
Strawberry Mousse 111
Streaky Spinach Salad ... 92
Stuffed Beef Capsicums . 57
Sumac and Orange Salad Dressing 70
Sweet Potato Truffles ... 102

T

Tamarind Chicken 58
Tamarind Tofu 59
Tofu Ginger Curry with Beans and Capsicum 60
Tofu Stir Fry 61
Tofu Tagine 62
Turkey burgers 63

V

Vegetarian Miso Soup 21
Vietnamese Coconut Dressing 71

W

Warm Summer Veg and Sumac Salad 93

Z

Zucchini and Leek Scramble 12
Zucchini Fettuccine 64
Zucchini Fritters 94
Zucchini, Fennel and Mint Salad 95
Zucchini, Haloumi and Herb Tarts 65

www.ingramcontent.com/pod-product-compliance
Lightning Source LLC
Chambersburg PA
CBHW040553010526
44110CB00054B/2672